The Structure of Digital Computing

FROM MAINFRAMES TO BIG DATA

BY

ROBERT L. GROSSMAN

OPEN DATA PRESS LLC
2012

Published by Open Data Press LLC
400 Lathrop Ave, Suite 90
River Forest, IL 60305, USA

First Printing: June, 2012

Library of Congress Control Number: 2012908445

ISBN 978-1-936298-00-6

To my wonderful wife.

Contents

1 The Five Eras of Computing   **1**
- 1.1 Introduction 1
- 1.2 The Main Themes 2
- 1.3 A Billion IP Addresses 5
- 1.4 The SAD History of Computing 9
- 1.5 Why Symbols Matter 11
- 1.6 Algorithms as Recipes 15
- 1.7 Computing Devices 17
- 1.8 Case Study: Slide Rule 19
- 1.9 From Mainframes to Devices 23
- 1.10 Mainframe Era 26
- 1.11 Case Study: Punch Cards 27
- 1.12 Personal Computer Era 28
- 1.13 The Web Era 30
- 1.14 Case Study: SMTP 31
- 1.15 Clouds of Devices 34
- 1.16 Case Study: Routers 36
- 1.17 The First Half Century of Computing . . . 38
- 1.18 The Commoditization of Data 43

2 Commoditization   **45**
- 2.1 Christmas and Easter 45
- 2.2 The Commoditization of Time 47
- 2.3 The Commoditization of Space 49
- 2.4 Moore's Law 52
- 2.5 Commoditization is All Around Us 54
- 2.6 The Doubling Game 58

i

2.7	Transforming Technologies	61
2.8	Storage and Johnson's Law	62
2.9	Bandwidth and Gilder's Law	66
2.10	Software and Stallman's Law	67
2.11	Data and the Bermuda Principles	74
2.12	Network Effects	75

3 Technical Innovation vs. Market Clutter **81**

3.1	Innovation vs. Clutter	81
3.2	Approximating Solutions to Equations . . .	83
3.3	Case Study: Business Intelligence	87
3.4	Views of Technical Innovation	88
3.5	The Imperative to be in the Upper Right .	91
3.6	Why Clutter Is Inevitable	93
3.7	Who Clutters	96
3.8	Sources of Clutter: Features	98
3.9	Case Study: Databases	101
3.10	Case Study: Searching for Primes	109
3.11	Case Study: Routing Packets	111

4 Technology Adoption Cycles **119**

4.1	Forces Effecting Technology Adoption . . .	119
4.2	The Basic Equation of Marketing	122
4.3	Getting to Main Street	127
4.4	Case Study: The Nike Pegasus	130
4.5	Technology Roadmaps	133
4.6	Case Study: Clusters	137
4.7	Context	140
4.8	Case Study: Relational Databases	145
4.9	Technology Pain Points	149
4.10	Case Study: Adoption of Linux	156

5 The Era of Data **161**

5.1	Introduction	161
5.2	Thinking about Big Data	162
5.3	The Commoditization of Data	164
5.4	The Data Gap	168
5.5	Extracting Knowledge from Data	172

5.6   Kepler's Law and Brahe's Data   178
5.7   Pearson's Law   182
5.8   The Bermuda Principles   188
5.9   World Population   190
5.10 The Shape of Data   193
5.11 Case Study: Consumer Databases   199
5.12 Creating Digital Data   203
5.13 Using Data to Make Decisions   207
5.14 Case Study: Mammograms   211
5.15 Events, Profiles and Alerts   214
5.16 Case Study: NASA's EOS   219

Notes   **225**

References   **249**

Preface

This book is about the structure of digital computing: what is significant, what is novel, what endures, and why it is all so confusing. The book tries to balance two point of views: digital computing as viewed from a business perspective, where the focus is on marketing and selling, and digital computing from a more technical perspective, where the focus is on developing new technology.

My goal was to write a short book about digital computing that takes a long term point of view and integrates to some extent these two perspectives.

The book is shaped by my personal experience in these two worlds: From 1996–2001, I was the Founder and the CEO of a company called Magnify, Inc. that developed and marketed software for managing and analyzing big data. Prior to this, from 1988–1996, I was faculty member at the University of Illinois at Chicago (UIC), where I did research on data intensive and distributed computing. From 1996–2010, I remained at UIC as a part time faculty member.

I wrote the sections in this book over an approximately eight year period from 2001 to 2008, with most of the writing done during 2001–2003. I have left the older sections by and large as they were originally written.

Although there have been some changes since 2003 (for example, computers are faster, there are more web sites, and phones are smarter), hopefully as the book will make clear, at a more fundamental level, we are still on the same fifty or so year trajectory today that we were on in 2003.

Robert L. Grossman

Chapter 1

The Five Eras of Computing

1.1 Introduction

This book is about the structure of digital computing: it is concerned with what is significant, what is novel, what endures, and why it is all so confusing.

Computing and communication technologies have gotten a bad name for being hard to predict and difficult to understand. In this book, I take the opposing point of view: that many of the most important phenomena that underlie computing have been remarkably regular and predictable over the past fifty years.

For example, the remarkable growth of processing power exemplified by Moore's Law has followed a regular pattern for over forty years. To put it simply, for most applications, processing power is a commodity and no harder to get than other commodities, such as electrical power. What is sometimes not appreciated is that a variety of other underlying processes that form the basis for today's computational and communications infrastructure have also been commoditized. For example, software and network bandwidth have been commoditized and show a similar regularity.

1

On the other hand, it is easy to lose sight of this regularity and predictability given the market clutter created by the many players with financial interests in computing and related fields. One of themes of this book is that technical innovation is generally masked by market clutter.

Understanding technology is often confused with the challenge of predicting which of the several thousand technology vendors will be around in five years and what their sales and profitability will be. This is a much harder problem and not one of the subjects of this book. It may be helpful to think of the survival of a vendor over five years as being modeled by a random walk, in much the same way that the stock market is often modeled by a random walk.

True computing innovations have a beauty and a longevity that creates regularity and simplicity in the historical narrative of computing. Although technical innovations are rare and cannot be predicted, they are usually recognized relatively quickly.

In this book, we try to focus on some of the underlying ideas and principles which have been fundamental drivers for computing and communications technology. These tend to be simple, rather than complex; long-lived, rather than short-lived; and easy to understand, but not easy to anticipate. These drivers have broad applicability rather than narrow applicability. Although they may have been introduced by individuals, they are brought to market by a variety of vendors using a variety of business models over a number of business cycles.

1.2   The Main Themes

> Everything should be made as simple as possible, but no simpler.
>
> ―――――――――――――――――――――――――――――――――――――
>
> Albert Einstein

This book has five main themes:

Theme 1. Our computing environment is shaped by commoditization, which governs the progress from one computing era to the next. The most familiar example of commoditization is Moore's law describing the rapid increase in power of integrated circuits at the same time that the unit cost has been stable or decreased. More generally, commoditization is the phenomenon in which unit capacity of a core technology grows exponentially, while unit cost is stable or decreases.

In this book we also examine the commoditization of several other critical technologies including storage, networking, and software. One of the themes in this book is that the commoditization of a handful of critical technologies has shaped our computing and communications infrastructure. We call these transforming technologies. Most other computing related technologies merely fill in the details.

The process of adopting and using transforming technologies is regular, lasts for decades, and is relatively easy to forecast. It is also not new. The printing press commoditized books and the telephone commoditized global person to person communication.

Chapter 1 provides an introduction to five different eras of computing, each one shaped by the commoditization of a different component of technology. Chapter 2 discusses commoditization in more detail.

Theme 2. Technical innovation is rare. It is also difficult to predict. Although technical innovation is important and critical, given its rarity, there is ample time to detect it and to understand it when it does occur.

You can think of innovation as being at the bottom of an inverted pyramid. Look it this way: A technical innovation requires at least 10 engineering advances. A hundred companies will try to bring products to market commercializing these advances. These companies over the lifetime of the products will produce 1000 marketing campaigns. Analysts and pundits will write 10,000 articles analyzing these campaigns and products. It is more efficient to understand the single innovation than to deconstruct the 10,000 articles.

Theme 3. Market clutter is rampant. The large number of players with financial stakes in technology produces a large amount of market clutter. It is hard to see through the market clutter. Pundits and industry analysts are part of the system and instead of helping, they make things worse. There is not much to do about this except to ignore it.

As already mentioned, in this book we tend to view the survival of a technology company over a five year period as a random walk: looking at five year intervals, some technology vendors will grow, some will shrink, and some will be absorbed by other vendors; but to first order, which vendor does which can best be modeled as random walk.

Chapter 3 is about the rarity of technical innovation and the confusion caused by market clutter.

Theme 4. Technology takes time. The process by which technology is created and adopted takes years. The process begins in the laboratory and ends with sales and marketing. This process is relatively well understood and relatively regular. On the other hand, the particular vendors that bring a new technology to market are not so easy to predict. Which vendors survive and which fail is perhaps best viewed as a random walk, as we have mentioned. The adoption of new technology is complicated by several different cycles involved: technology adoption cycles usually last a decade or more, while the life cycle of many technology companies is 3-7 years, and marketing cycles and fashions last 1 to 2 years. You can think of this as a tricycle with three different size wheels. Steering is obviously quite hard.

Chapter 4 is about technology adoption cycles.

Theme 5. We are entering the era of big data. We are currently entering an era defined by the commoditization of data. More precisely, over the next decade or so, we will be entering a new era of discovery driven by vast amounts of new data being produced and archived. From a broad historical perspective, having a surplus of unanalyzed data is unusual. For example, Darwin spent 17 years collecting data before publishing one of his papers. On the other hand, today an individual with a laptop and a web connection can try to create new drugs by accessing human genetic sequences, three dimensional protein data, and the chemical properties of various compounds. All this is available from the web today at no cost.

Chapter 5 is about this emerging era of data.

How the book is organized. The chapters are meant to be read in order. As just mentioned, Chapter 1 provides a framework for understanding the most important broad trends in computing. Chapter 2 is about commoditization. Chapter 3 is about the rarity of innovation and the prevalence of market clutter. It contains lots of examples, the purpose of which is to give the reader some practice so that it is easier to separate technical innovation from market clutter. Chapter 4 describes the pattern with which new technology is typically adopted by the market and the many years this usually requires. Chapter 5 is about the Era of Big Data.

Each chapter contains several extended examples and case studies, some of which are quite detailed. Feel free to skim or to ignore the ones that you don't find interesting. These examples and case studies are included since many people find it easiest to learn through concrete examples.

1.3   Case Study: A Billion IP Addresses

When you use your home computer to buy an airline ticket on the web site www.united.com, your computer looks up the web site www.united.com to get the number 209.87.-112.90. This is called an *IP address* and in some ways is somewhat similar to a telephone number. The current format for IP addresses was defined in 1981 and provided roughly 4 billion of them. Since the 1981 world population

```
 9  44 40 40   209.247.34.166   internap-ne.chicago1.level3.net
10  38 37 37   64.94.32.11      border6.po1-bbnet1.chg.pnap.net
11  49 40 41   64.94.34.74      mypoints10.border6.chg.pnap.net
12  45 40 40   209.87.127.111   -
13  42 40 43   209.87.112.90    www.united.com
```

Figure 1.1: The Linux command traceroute provides the IP addresses of intermediate points between your computer and hosts on the Internet, such as www.united.com. This is fragment of a traceroute to www.united.com, showing the last portion of the route to www.united.com. The fifth column is the IP address of the intermediate points along the way to www.united.com.

was roughly 4.5 billion, since only a handful of people had access to computers, and since only some of these had network access, this seem a reasonable number of addresses.

To connect to the Internet, a company such as United Airlines needs an IP address such as 209.87.112.90. Once it has an IP address, it can provide a variety of services, such as serving web pages describing flights between Chicago and Hawaii and offering airline tickets for sale.

Beginning in 1999, a new type of Internet address became available, called IPv6. An example of an IPv6 address is

```
1080:0:0:0:8:800:200C:417A.
```

IPv6 addresses are longer than IPv4 addresses. IPv4 addresses are 32 bits long, while IPv6 addresses are 128 bits long.

Today, not only can computers connect to the Internet, but so can mobile phones. This means that it is useful for a mobile phone to have an IP number. For over a decade it has been clear that there were not enough IPv4 addresses for each device, such as a mobile telephone, to have its own IPv4 number. The IPv6 addresses were introduced in part so that each device could have its own IP number and easily connect to the Internet.

A manufacturer of mobile telephones, such as Nokia or Ericsson, is assigned large blocks of IPv6 addresses to burn in to the telephones they build. Blocks are assigned in units called /48's. For example, Nokia would request a /48 from European Registry for the delegation of Internet Numbers or ERIN. The interesting thing is that a /48 has enough IP numbers to set up 2^{16} separate networks, with each network having as many as 2^{64} separate computers or other IP devices [62].

Since the world population is about 6 billion (or about 2^{30}, this may seem somewhat excessive. On the other hand, there were about 1.18 billion new telephones sold in 2008, about 39% of the them by Nokia [109]. Today, we are in the midst of a transition from a computing infrastructure in which computers are connected to form networks that are in turn aggregated to form the Internet, to an infrastructure in which mobile devices supplying services are connected to form networks that are in turn connected to create clouds of services. A Nokia phone may require several IP addresses, each for a separate service in the cloud, such as talking, browsing the web, GPS location, etc. From this perspective, a billion addresses doesn't go as far as once did.

The Internet interconnects millions of different networks and billions of different computers and devices. Each computer which is directly on the Internet has a unique IP address. The simplest of are obtained by concatenating a network ID and a host ID. The network ID identifies which network it is on, while the host ID distinguishes different computers on the same network.

Actually, it is a bit more complicated. Just as some large offices use private branch exchanges (PBXs) so that individual phones have extension numbers and not unique telephone numbers, many large companies use a similar scheme so that the company itself has an IP address and individual companies have what are essentially extension numbers, which are used within the company's internal network.

Here is another way to think about the transition from

IPV4 to IPV6. IPV4 provides about 4 billion different addresses, which was originally more than enough to create a
world wide network of computers, but which today is running out of space. IPV6 provides about 340 trillion, trillion,
trillion (3.4×10^{38}) addresses, which is enough today to create a world wide network of devices, but which in twenty
years may not be enough. With IPV6 there are enough addresses so that your phones, games, cars, and cameras can
each have several different addresses.

The transition from a world wide network of computers
to a world wide network of devices is natural and grad-
ual and part of broader transition that is over fifty years
old. Indeed, over the past fifty years, computer hardware,
computer software, and networking have progressed in a
relatively predictable fashion over a trajectory which will
soon create a world in which your cell phone and car are
just as much part of a network as your Gmail account.

If this seems surprising, it is simply because news about
computing is reported as consisting of a series of breakthroughs. In fact, computing can more fruitfully be thought
of as a trajectory in which the slope changes from time to
time as the result of innovation. Innovation is hard to predict but is quickly recognized and does not change the fundamental pattern. This doesn't mean everything is easy to
predict in computing. For example, predicting which company will supply the component technology for your cell
phone and car is not so easy. Predicting vendors in this
fashion perhaps may be best considered as the result of a
random walk. News about which vendors are ahead and
which are behind is part of the market clutter which makes
learning about technology confusing. On the other hand,
unless you have invested in one of these companies, you
don't care all that much as long as one company survives.

We are currently in an era of computing dominated by
web browsers surfing the Internet. Over the next decade
we will transition to an era of computing in which large
numbers of devices will all connect to networks, many of
which will be wireless, and all of which will be able to com-

municate with each other. Over the past decade we have emerged from an era of computing characterized by PCs using office applications, such as word processors and spread sheets. Prior to that, computing was dominated by terminals connected to mainframes. These four eras span over half a century. From this perspective, change has been relatively easy to predict. This is the perspective of this book.

In this chapter, we describe these four major eras of computing that span the past fifty years in more detail. We will also describe an emerging fifth era of computing in which data and information will become just as commoditized as have computer cycles, storage, bandwidth and software in the proceeding eras.

1.4 The SAD History of Computing

The river where you set your foot just now is gone — those waters giving way to this, now this.

Heraclitus

What has been, that will be; what has been done, that will be done. Nothing is new under the sun. Even the thing of which we say, "See, this is new!" has already existed in the ages that preceded us.

Ecclesiastes

In this book, we take a broad perspective on computing and communication, trying to understand digital computing and communication from the perspective of decades, rather than the perspective of a media cycle, in which there is pressure for each new print edition or each new broadcast to announce something innovative. To do this, in Section 1.9 we will divide computing and communication technologies into five eras: the mainframe era, the personal computer era, the web era, the device era, and the data era.

Before we begin though, it is instructive to take an even longer perspective and to divide computing and communicating technologies into several epochs, the last of which is the digital epoch. (Think of epochs as much longer than eras.)

From this broader perspective, progress in computing and communications can be viewed along three dimensions: the *symbols* used, the *algorithms* which govern how we manipulate the symbols in order to compute something, and the *devices* used to manipulate the symbols. It might be helpful to remember the acronym **SAD** for **S**ymbols, **A**lgorithms and **D**evices.

A good example of this perspective is provided by the slide rule. The symbols used by slide rules are the same symbols that children learn in elementary school today. What is important to remember is that the positional number system in which $1402 = 1 \times 1000 + 4 \times 100 + 0 \times 10 + 2$ was not available to the Greeks, and was only fully developed in India during the 9th century. Because of this, computation was much more difficult for the Greeks.

Algorithms for multiplying and dividing numbers using slide rules rely on two formulas involving logarithms that developed in the 17th century and turn multiplication and division into addition and subtraction.

A simple slide rule consists of two ruled pieces of wood, one of which can be moved relative to the other. This is the device and it is a simple but effective analog computer. The slide rule as a computing device is so elegant and effective that it dominated computation for over 300 years.

As another example, today's digital computers use symbols representing binary numbers, employ algorithms that add, multiply, and perform other operations on these symbols, and rely on devices that implement these algorithms using transistors and integrated circuits. Progress is typically measured simply by how many operations can be performed in one second. In some sense this is like measuring the beauty of a painting by how many brushstrokes are used.

From a broad (SAD) perspective, as we will see, much of today's computing infrastructure is based upon symbols from the 18th century, algorithms from the 19th century, and devices from the 20th century. Of course the marketing is from the 21st century, so people today can be proud of something.

1.5 Why Symbols Matter

All is Number.

Attributed to Pythagoras

Euclid alone
Has looked on Beauty bare.

Edna St. Vincent Millay (1892–1950)

Computation is intimately tied up with the symbols we use. Symbols and computation are so interwoven that it is easy to take for granted the power provided by innovative symbols. In this section, we discuss a few examples of how innovations involving symbols can dramatically simplify computations.

By the time a student today enters high school, she has written both large numbers (e.g. $299,792,458$) and fractions (e.g. 3.1415926535) using positional notation; she has used scientific notation (e.g. 6.38×10^{27}) for computations; and she has used symbols to represent numbers (e.g. let x be a number whose square is 16) and geometric quantities (e.g. let x be the radius of a circle whose circumference is 10).

What a student doesn't always appreciate is how relatively recent some of these innovations are: for example, the transition in Europe from Roman numerals to the positional Hindu-Arabic system took several centuries and did not become common until the 16th century; logarithms were not introduced until the 17th century; and symbols to represent numeric and geometric quantities were also introduced in the 17th century.

In classical antiquity, the Babylonians, Greeks, Egyptians, and Romans each used different symbols and number systems. The Babylonians used a positional number system with a base of sixty, which we have inherited to this day for measurements involving navigation, astronomy, and time. For example, there are sixty seconds in a minute and sixty minutes in an hour. The sun was observed to require about 360 days to complete a circle, so a circle was divided into 360 degrees, and each degree was divided into 60 minutes ('), each minute into 60 seconds ("), and each second into sixty thirds ("').

Archimedes (c. 287 BC – c. 212 BC) did not have the use of the positional number system. He wrote a paper called the Sand Reckoner in which he tried to estimate the number of grains of sand that would fill the earth. It was not an easy computation and would have been much simpler if he had used the positional number system that we take for granted today.

The Greeks during the time of Archimedes used the letters to represent number as follows: $1, 2, 3, \ldots, 9$ were represented by the letters alpha through theta; $10, 20, 30, \ldots 90$ were represented by the letters iota through koppa (koppa is not part of the current Greek alphabet); $100, 200, 300, \ldots, 900$ were represented by the letters rho through san (san is not part of the current Greek alphabet). For example, the number 222 was written sigma kappa beta.

To represent numbers greater than 999, subscripts and superscripts were used. For example, adding the Greek letter iota as a subscript or superscript to the letters alpha, beta, ..., theta, produced the numbers 1000, 2000, $\ldots, 9000$.

Rules for adding and multiplying using this type of alphabetic system were more complicated than the familiar rules today. Just think for a moment how hard it would be to estimate the number of grains of sand in the earth using this number system.

Numbers in the fifth century BC were thought of geometrically. This way thinking can be seen in Euclid's El-

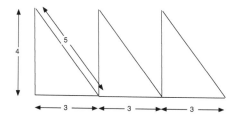

Figure 1.2: The Greek Parthenon is 69.5 meters longs, 30.88 meters wide and 13.72 meters tall, exactly the same proportions that you get if you take three 3x4 rectangles and lay them end to end as indicated. Note that the length of the diagonal of a 3x4 rectangle is 5.

ements, which captured the geometry of the 4th century B.C. Greeks. This was a tremendous achievement and provided fundamental insights and algorithms for a variety of different problems, both theoretical and practical.

A good example of how the Greeks viewed numbers as geometric lengths and ratios is provided by the Parthenon [115]. The Parthenon is 69.5 meters long, 30.88 meters wide, and 13.72 meters high. This means that the ratio of the width to the length is 30.88/69.5 or about 4/9, while the ratio of the height to the width is 13.72/30.88 or about 4/9. These are the dimensions you would get if you took three rectangles of length 3×4 and placed them side by side, as in the diagram below. Note that the diagonal of a 3×4 rectangle is of length 5, since by the Pythagorean Theorem $3 \times 3 + 4 \times 4 = 5 \times 5$.

Another significant advance in computing which is easy to take for granted is the introduction in the seventeenth century of symbols for unknown quantities, such as the variable x. With these types of symbols, equations such as 2.2 x = 32.8 could be easily represented, as could geometric objects such as the circles, ellipses, and hyperbolas.

Just as today's positional number system enables com-

putations that would be simply impractical with the Greek
or Roman number system, it is instructive to imagine new
types of symbols that might provide a similar advantage
over today's use of binary symbols to represent positional
numbers.

Here is a simple example. For over thirty years, computer scientists have been building systems for what is
called *symbolic computation.* These systems manipulate
symbolic as opposed to numeric entities. Using such a system, one can multiply two polynomials like $x + 2$ and $x + 3$
to compute their product $x^2 + 5x + 6$. Simple versions of
these systems are now found in calculators.

Another example is in logic programming, where systems work with assertions and rules to draw conclusions
from them.

In Chapter 5, we discuss some of the ways multimedia
digital data, such as images and audio files, are created.
Working with these digitally requires symbols for encoding
images and sounds, as well as devices for taking light waves
and audio waves and producing discrete symbols, such as
the symbols (135, 206, 235) or #82CAFF to represent the
color sky blue in HTML documents.

Today we use symbols from different alphabets to form
expressions which fill files to record a wide variety of things,
including shapes (vector graphics SVG files), colors (JPEG
files), sounds (MP3 files), and video (MPEG and DVD
files).

From this perspective, our ability to compute depends
critically upon the richness of the symbols we use and the
power of the algorithms we use for transforming the symbols.

1.6 Algorithms as Recipes
for Manipulating Symbols

> Science is what we understand well enough to explain to
> a computer. Art is everything else we do.

> Donald Knuth

Having fixed a collection of symbols, the next question is what do we do with them? What are the rules and systems for manipulating them? Algorithms may be thought of as formal procedures for manipulating symbols. For many problems, such as predicting the trajectory of a projectile, factoring prime numbers, or predicting tomorrow's weather, algorithms affect the speed of computation just as much, or more, than the hardware of the computing platform.

It is easy to explain the basic idea of an algorithm using an example. Recall that x is called a square of a in case x times x is equal to a. For example, 2 is the square root of 4, 3 is the square root of 9, and 5 is the square root of 25.

Here is a simple algorithm for computing the square root of a number a.

1. Begin with a guess x for the square root.

2. Replace x by the average of x and a/x.

3. Go to Step 2.

Here are some approximations to the square roots of 2, 5 and 5, 934, 939 using a five line Python program that you can find in the notes:


```
sqrt of 2
1.5
1.41666666667
1.41421568627
```

```
1.41421356237
1.41421356237
...

sqrt of 5
2.25
2.23611111111
2.23606797792
2.2360679775
2.2360679775
...


sqrt of 5,934,939
1483735.75
741869.874999
370938.937486
185477.46863
92754.7333983
46409.3593468
23268.6208599
11761.8413875
6133.21703089
3550.44423902
2611.0244305
2442.02762481
2436.18004142
2436.17302342
2436.17302341
2436.17302341
...
```

The three dots indicate that the last number repeats.

As can be seen from this example, an algorithm consists of a series of steps each of which can be carried out explicitly once the previous steps are completed. More or less, one can think of an algorithm as anything that can be expressed by a computer program.

The notes for this section contains another algorithm called Newton's Method, which can be used to find the solutions of a wide class of equations.

1.7   Computing Devices

[Mathematical] Tables have been with us for some 4500 years. For at least the last two millennia they have been the main calculation aid, and in dynamic form remain important today. Their importance as a central component and generator of scientific advance over that period can be underestimated by sheer familiarity. Like other apparently simple technological or conceptual advances (such as writing, numerals, or money) their influence on history is very deep.

The History of Mathematical Tables: From Sumer to Spreadsheets, edited by M. Campbell-Kelly, M. Croarken, R. Flood and E. Robson.

It is easy to take paper, pens and pencils for granted, but they are important computing devices. Twenty five hundred years ago, Babylonian computation was done in clay, Chinese computation was done using bark and bamboo, and Egyptian computation was done using papyrus.

For perspective, Homer's Iliad and Odyssey were not initially written down, but passed on instead as an oral tradition. Indeed, they were composed at a time when the Greek alphabet was still emerging and when papyrus was scarce.

Papyrus was an early form of paper made from the papyrus plant, which grew mainly in Egypt and had to be imported by other regions. Egyptian papyri document some of the earliest algorithms that we know of. For example, what is sometime called the Rhind papyrus was written about 1650 BC by the scribe Ahmes. It is about 20 feet long by 1 foot wide and contains 87 problems, including problems requiring multiplying numbers and working with fractions. For example, Problem 4 shows how to divide 7 loaves of bread between 10 men.

Parchment, which is made from animal skins, was also used for writing, and may have been invented in part because of the difficulty obtaining papyrus outside of Egypt. Parchment can be made from a number of animal skins, including those of calves, sheep or goats. Although humans have used animal skins since paleolithic times, the preparation and use of animal skins for writing is much more recent. Parchment was invented about third or second century BCE in Pergamum (modern day Turkey). Parchment became generally available in the Hellenistic world during the first century AD. Parchment was used extensively through the middle ages, and is still sometimes used to this day for diplomas or other special documents.

Euclid's Elements is one of the most important books containing Greek mathematics. Early versions were probably written in papyrus, with later versions written in parchment. The earliest version still extant is in parchment and was written in 888 AD, almost 1200 years after the original.

Paper was invented in China about 105 AD. Paper is made from fibers extracted from wood pulp, from trees such as spruce or pine trees. Paper can also be made from fibers extracted from other sources, such as cotton or rice. In Europe, paper began to replace parchment during the middle ages.

Moving from clay and wood to parchment and paper was one of the first significant advances in computing devices. On the other hand, the Babylonian computations preserved on clay proved to be more durable, which is why we know a bit more about how the Babylonians computed during this time than how some of their contemporaries did.

Paper is still a wonderful device for computing. It is one of the most flexible devices and supports not only numerical computation, but also computation involving algebraic, geometric and logical symbols. Over the last few hundred years, it has been augmented by wooden devices, such as slide rules; mechanical devices, such as adding machines built from gears; and electronic devices, such as a calculators and computers built from vacuum tubes, transistors, and integrated circuits.

There is no reason to expect the development of new computing devices to slow down. Not only do integrated circuits continue to improve, but so does the exploration of novel devices, such as devices that use genes to compute or that exploit quantum mechanics.

1.8   Case Study: Slide Rule

> When I was research head of General Motors and wanted a problem solved, I'd place a table outside the meeting room with a sign: LEAVE SLIDE RULES HERE! If I didn't do that, I'd find some engineer reaching for his slide rule.
>
> Charles F. Kettering (1876-1958)

The slide rule is a computing device that enormously sped up the computation of a sequence of multiplications and divisions, as well as a variety of other computations, such as extracting square roots. Slides rules were introduced in the 17th century and were an important computing device for over three hundred years, a reign significantly longer than the modern digital computer.

Prior to slide rules, the device most often used for mathematical computations was probably a mathematical table. Mathematical tables are one of the earliest computing devices. We have examples of tables used by Babylonians dating from about 2000 BC.

Tables are still used in mathematics to this day, and so are in the running for one of the computing devices with the longest staying power. Tables are easy to use. For example, using the table of sines below, we can read off the sine of 80 degrees as 0.98481 by reading the table from left to right. We can also read the table from right to left to see that the

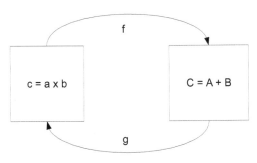

Step 1. Compute A = f(a), B= f(B)
Step 2. Compute C = A + B
Step 3. Compute c = g(C)

Figure 1.3: The first idea underlying the slide rule is that there are certain functions (f and g in the diagram) that transform multiplication and division into addition and subtraction. John Napier discovered such a pair of functions in the early 17th century.

number whose sine is -0.34202 is 200 degrees. Reading the table from right to left computes a function which undoes the sine (the function is called the arcsine). To compute the sine of 50 degrees, we know from the table that it is between 0.64279 and 0.86603 (the sines of 40 degrees and 60 degrees). If we take the midpoint of these two numbers we get 0.75441, which is close but not exactly the sine of 50 degrees which is 0.76604. Over the years, a number of formulas have been developed to interpolate between two values in a table to get more accurate answers.

There are two basic ideas underlying the slide rule:

The first idea is that certain functions can reduce multiplication and division to addition and subtraction. In 1614, John Napier (1550-1617) introduced a very nice function (a variant of today's logarithm function) with the property of reducing multiplications to additions. See Figure 1.3.

The second idea is due to Edmund Gunter (1581-1626).

degrees	sine
0	0.00000
20	0.34202
40	0.64279
60	0.86603
80	0.98481
100	0.98481
120	0.86603
140	0.64279
160	0.34202
180	0.00000
200	-0.34202
220	-0.64279
240	-0.86603
260	-0.98481
280	-0.98481
300	-0.86603
320	-0.64279
340	-0.34202
360	0.00000

Table 1.1: This is a simple mathematical table. If you read from left to right, you can compute the sine of various numbers. If you read from right to left, you can compute another function, called arcsine, that is the inverse of the sine function.

Figure 1.4: Edmund Gunter positioned numbers along a piece of wood according to their logarithms. The Gunter scale was used by seamen to simplify computations for navigation.

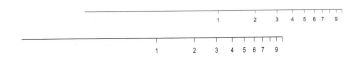

Figure 1.5: About 1625, William Oughtred put together two Gunter scales, allowing one to slide next to the other to create the slide rule.

His idea was to create a scale on wood in which numbers were marked according to their logarithms. See Figure 1.4

About 1625, William Oughtred (1575-1660) put together two Gunter scales so that one could slide next to the other, creating the slide rule. Slide rules were one of the staples of computation until the introduction of handheld calculators in the 1970s.

To end the section, let us try to characterize the slide rule from the symbols-algorithms-devices (SAD) perspective:

First, let us think of the slide rule as a device. From this perspective, it was a true revolution. Prior to slide rules, computations were done using tables, for example, tables of sines, cosines, square roots, and logarithms. The slide rule allowed one device (mathematical tables) and several manual look-ups to be replaced by another device (the slide rule) and two operations (moving one wooden rule with respect to the other) and moving a reference line along the two slides. In other words, this elegant device replaced large mathematical tables and error prone manual look-ups. In fact, multiple tables could be encoded on the same device, so that a single slide rule could replace tables of square roots, cube roots, and logarithms.

Second, consider the algorithms involved. From this perspective, the slide rule is less innovative. Indeed, the algorithms used for a slide rule are essentially the same algorithms used previously with mathematical tables. The first algorithm is a simple look-up (reading a table from left to right) or reverse look up (reading a table from right to left). The second algorithm is using a function like the logarithm to replace multiplications and divisions by additions and subtractions.

Third, consider the symbols involved. Again, from this perspective, the symbols used in mathematical tables and the symbols used in slide rules are essentially the same: positional numbers (like 1.414213562).

Although the computing devices we describe next don't have the staying power of mathematical tables (4000+ years) or slide rules (300+ years), they do have the advantage that they can also be used for playing music and writing emails to your family and friends. On the other hand, neither mathematical tables nor slide rules require batteries or electricity and both function perfectly well a decade after production.

1.9   From Mainframes to Devices

The longer you look back, the further you can look forward.

Winston Churchill

It is difficult to tell a short-sighted man how to get
somewhere. Because you cannot say to him: "Look at
that church tower ten miles away and go in that
direction."

Ludwig Wittgenstein

One of the themes of this book is that digital computing
for the past fifty years or so has been shaped in large part by
the process of commoditization. To understand commoditization better, it is useful to divide the past fifty years into
four eras, consisting of overlapping 20 year periods.

1. The Mainframe Era (1965 - 1985). In 1965, IBM
   shipped the System 360, its first computer based on
   integrated circuits. By 1968, it had installed over
   14,000 System 360 systems, at an average price of
   over $1,000,000 per system, generating over $14 billion dollars of revenue for IBM. During the Mainframe Era, computing cycles were limited. Departments were built around the mainframes to operate
   them, ration their cycles, and provide services to the
   users.

2. The Personal Computer (PC) Era (1980-2000). In
   1977, Apple, Commodore and Tandy began selling
   personal computers. In 1981, IBM entered the market, effectively setting the standard, with a business
   model which encouraged third party manufacturers.
   For example, Compaq shipped its first IBM clone in
   1983 and set a record by selling $111 million of PCs,
   one of the largest first year product sales in the history of American business. By the end of this era,
   over 50 percent of the workers in some metropolitan areas had PCs. PCs had also became building
   blocks for specialized computing needs: for example,
   rather than build specialized devices for supercomputing, supercomputers were being built by putting
   together hundreds or thousands of PCs into what are

called clusters. During the PC Era, computer hardware became a commodity.

3. The Web Era (1995-2015). In 1993, Mosaic, the first graphics based web browser, was released. It was developed at the National Center for Supercomputing Applications at the University of Illinois in Urbana Champaign. In 1995, NSF turned over the networking backbone for the Internet to commercial vendors and, at the same time, introduced a research network called the very High Speed Backbone Network Service or vBNS, that became the foundation for the next generation of the Internet. By 1996, the number of hosts on the Internet exceeded 10 million. By 2000, the number exceeded 75 million hosts. With the Internet, it became much easier to develop and deploy software applications that essentially used the Internet as the operating system. Companies began to give away software. For example, Hotmail was a free email program and had over 30 million users two and half years after its launch in 1996. During the Web Era, software became a commodity.

4. The Device Era (2005-2025). There is no generally accepted name for the post-web era. In this era, PCs connected to the web will be supplemented by a wide variety of networked devices, many of which are wireless. These devices include mobile phones, personal digital assistants (PDAs), devices for listening to music, cars emitting diagnostic information, cameras, home stereos, as well as a variety of other devices not yet prototyped. At the beginning of the device era, wireless Internet is available at coffee shops and bookstores, and some cities are providing free wireless Internet. During the Device Era, networks will become a commodity.

Dividing the digital age into four eras simply provides convenient markers for certain inflection points. For example, although the web era is defined as the twenty year period from 1995-2015, the roots of the web era date back at least to the sixties. For example, the first paper on packet switching, which is one of the main ideas for the Internet's network architecture, was published by Leonard Kleinrock from MIT in 1961. In 1967, Larry Roberts of ARPA organized the first meeting to design what would become ARPANET, the predecessor of the Internet. In 1969, ARPANET began operations with nodes at UCLA, the Stanford Research Institute (SRI), the University of California at Santa Barbara (UCSB) and the University of Utah.

In other words, the divisions between the different eras should be thought of as simply convenient markers denoting a time in which the prior era's technology is widely diffused, and the next era is well on its way. For example, by 1996, near the beginning of the web era, there were over 10 million hosts on the Internet. By this time, your father and your grandfather were likely to have heard of the Internet.

1.10   The First Era: Mainframes

From today's viewpoint, life with the first computers seems to belong to a simpler, more romantic time: there was basically one type of computer — the mainframes — and one dominant company — IBM. Of course, if you look deeper, there were specialized computers for specialized purposes, and several companies trying to gain the dominant market share.

More importantly, though, the computing was centralized, and the control of the system was firmly in the hands of the professional computing staff. Individuals accessed information through terminals that were networked to the mainframe. To get new information from the system or old information presented in a new way, one submitted a written request which eventually either led to what was wanted or to a further request. On the positive side, the mainframe with its centralized structure meant that the information was secure and that operations were managed by professionals. One also knew who to blame when things went wrong.

During this period, mainframe computers primarily managed corporate level information, such as employee records, accounting data, and product data.

In a sense that will become clearer as we consider the second and third eras, the first era can be characterized as being hardware-limited. The challenge was to provide the appropriate hardware to the customer. Companies such as IBM, which provided this hardware and the associated services, grew to be quite large.

1.11 Case Study: Punch Cards

Old technologies are a bit like photographs — you never really throw them away, you just spend less time with them. In the second and third eras, the era of PCs and the Web, many companies still use mainframes for important business processes, such as the preparation of payrolls.

Not only are mainframes still critical in producing payrolls but so are punch cards. In the 1880's, the punch card was invented by Herman Hollerith to automate the US Census. Holes in a punch card are translated by a punch card reader into mechanical or electrical signals that can be counted or further processed.

One of the most common uses of punch cards was to compute payroll. For example, the garment industry used punch cards as follows. A punch card was created each time an individual working on a garment performed a particular operation in the manufacture of the garment. If a worker performed 100 operations per day for five days, this generated 500 punch cards. One hundred employees would generate 5000 punch cards per week, which would be tabulated to produce the week's payroll.

In the 1970's, disk drives began replacing the punch

cards as the main storage mechanism for data. Today, it is very difficult even to find a punch card reader. On the other hand, systems using them as the basic form of data entry still persist. In 2002, the New York Times ran a story describing how the 23,000 employees of the Los Angeles County Department of Health Services still use punch cards for their time card and payroll system [83]. Punch cards are still used because the system still works and moving all the hospitals and clinics to a new system would be too expensive.

In 1967, an estimated 260 billion punch cards were used in the US or 1,300 for each American. Today, there are only three companies in the US that manufacture punch cards. On the other hand, punch cards are still used for many voting machines, as became apparent in the 2000 Presidential election controversy.

1.12   The Second Era: PCs

The emergence of microprocessor-based computers ushered in a new era because for the first time hardware became a commodity. During this era, personal computers covered more and more desk tops. Companies that provided useful desktop applications such as word processors, spreadsheets, and databases grew. Hardware was distributed and computing was based on the client-server model in which larger systems (servers) provided data and information to smaller systems, such as personal computers (clients) networked to them.

Individuals could suddenly buy, install, and use desktop applications without the lengthy involvement of a centralized computing department. On the other hand, individuals were suddenly responsible for managing and servicing their desktop systems and protecting their desktop data.

The information on the desktop was, by and large, department level information generated by individuals: reports, presentations, budgets, and other work related data.

The VisiCalc spreadsheet was one of the first new types applications to be designed for the PC. VisiCalc was designed and developed by Dan Bricklin and Bob Frankston. Bricklin and Frankston formed Software Arts, Inc. on January 2, 1979, and worked out of their attics. There was very little infrastructure for developing applications on the PC in those days. The first version of VisiCalc was written for the Apple II in assembler, a low level language that required quite a bit of code for such things as reading input from the keyboard, saving information to a file, or reading information from a file. With higher level languages these days, these operations can all be done with a single line of code.

If you grew up using spreadsheets, it may be a bit difficult to imagine how business was conducted before they were introduced. The first business application of VisiCalc took place while Dan Bricklin was getting an MBA at the Harvard Business School in 1979. MBAs at Harvard learned about business through case studies. Bricklin used an early version of VisiCalc to analyze the Pepsi Challenge marketing campaign for the Pepsi Corporation case study. While the other students in the class used a Texas Instrument Business Analyst calculator, Bricklin used VisiCalc, allowing him to do five year forecasts and vary many of the assumptions. When the professor teaching the class asked Bricklin how he had done all the projections, Bricklin answered in a way that didn't disclose that he had used an entirely new type of product, since he wanted to keep the VisiCalc secret until it was closer to being released.

A few years later, spreadsheets would transform many business processes. For example, Kohlberg Kravis Roberts & Company, commonly referred to as KKR, is a New York City-based company that popularized the leveraged buyout. One of their secret weapons was using spreadsheets to analyze quickly the cash generated under various scenarios when the acquired company was split apart in different ways. This was very important, since KKR used the acquired company's own cash for the buyout, and financed the rest by issuing high yield (also known as junk) bonds.

In some sense, the PC Era was limited by the availability of the appropriate desktop software and the challenge was to provide this software to the customer. Companies such as Microsoft that met this challenge became the icons for this era.

1.13   The Third Era: The Web

A typical software application during the PC Era was Microsoft Word, a word processor. A typical software application in the Web Era is Google's GMail, an email program. Software from the PC Era resides on your desktop computer or your laptop. Software from the Web Era is often on another machine and you access it through a web browser over a network.

The significance of the world wide web is not only that one can click to bring up an interesting picture or that one can buy a book over the web, but rather that information and services from millions of servers on the network are just as easily available as if they were your own desktop PC.

The icons of this age are not the hardware vendors — IBM sold its PC business in 2004 — nor the software vendors — much of the software infrastructure, such as the Apache web server, is open source and not sold by a software vendor but instead developed by a distributed team of volunteers — but rather providers of web-based services, such as Amazon, eBay, and Google.

Think of it this way: someone buying a book on Amazon is more aware of how slow her network connection is than what the model of her PC is or which software vendor developed her web browser. Over a two year period, the book buyer will easily pay more for her DSL-based network connection (2 years x 12 months per year x 50 dollars per month or $1200) than for her PC clone ($800) or her open source Mozilla Fire Fox web browser ($0). During the web era, hardware and software are commodities, but network access and web based business services are still a scarce resource.

During the web era not only is network access a scarce commodity but so is information. This is a bit counter-intuitive, since suddenly not only is everything on your own computer accessible, but, via the web, so is much of the information on the computers of colleagues and strangers. The problem, though, is that this information is rarely organized well enough so that you can readily use it.

Think for a moment about how information is organized on your own desktop or laptop computer. For most of us, organizing information on our computer is put on a to-do list almost as frequently, and no more effectively, than losing ten extra pounds of weight. Suddenly, not only must your computer be organized, but so must the computers of all your colleagues, as well as those of strangers you have never met.

In other words, although the amount of digital data is growing, the amount of useful information is not keeping up. The technology to screen, sort, and extract useful information from large amounts of digital data is not yet ready for everyday use. This is the challenge of the next era. Companies that succeed with these challenges, such as Google, are candidates to be the icons of the next era.

1.14   Case Study: SMTP

This section contains a case study of the Internet protocol that powers email. An Internet protocol is roughly speaking a "language" that allows two computers on the Internet to communicate. There are a large number of different Internet protocols, including those that support email, web browsing, and setting up telephone calls over the Internet. Email is commonly considered as the *killer application* or killer app that sparked the adoption of the Internet among consumers.

Many users access email through an email application

such as Microsoft's Outlook or Outlook Express. Outlook is
a proprietary client that not only interfaces to proprietary
Microsoft products and services but also interfaces to open
protocols and services, such as the Simple Mail Transfer
Protocol or SMTP. Although most people have never heard
of it, SMTP is one of the main reasons that email became
a killer app.

SMTP is a computer-to-computer (C2C) protocol that
allows two computers on the Internet to exchange email
messages [126]. Here is an example from the original 1982
description of SMTP [126]:

```
S: MAIL FROM:
R: 250 OK

S: RCPT TO:
R: 250 OK

S: RCPT TO:
R: 550 No such user here

S: RCPT TO:
R: 250 OK

S: DATA
R: 354 Start mail input; end with .
S: Blah blah blah...
S: ...etc. etc. etc.
S: .
R: 250 OK
```

EMail is exchanged when an email client connects to a
SMTP server. The SMTP server is a computer that provides an Internet or web service. In particular it listens for
requests from SMTP clients. Clients include proprietary
Microsoft products such Outlook, as well as browser-based
email, such as those provided by Google, Yahoo or Hotmail.

In the computer-to-computer conversation above, Smith
(the sender S) at the computer alpha.arpa tries to send

email to Jones (the receiver R) at beta.arpa and Green
(the receiver R) at beta.arpa. He succeeds with Jones but
not with Green. The email is sent as an ASCII text stream.

The computer-to-computer conversation takes place between two different computer programs residing on two different nodes on the Internet without human intervention.
A special case is when both programs reside on the same
node. The conversation between the SMTP-Sender and the
SMTP-Receiver is pretty simple and consists of three steps.

In the first step, the SMTP-Sender sends a mail command:

```
MAIL  FROM:
```

This command tells the SMTP-Receiver that a new
message is being sent. The reverse path is used so that
the SMTP-Receiver can return a 250 OK reply after suc-
cessfully processing the command. In the second step, the
SMTP-Sender sends a RCPT command:

```
RCPT  FROM:
```

This command gives the address of the one recipient of
the message. If the SMTP-Receiver accepts the recipient,
it returns a "250 OK"; if not, it returns a "550 No such user
here". This step is repeated once for each user the message
is sent to.

In the third step, the SMTP-Sender sends a DATA command containing the message itself:

```
DATA
```

If the SMTP-Receiver accepts this commands it returns
a "354 Intermediate Reply". Once the SMTP-Sender receives the 354 command, it begins sending data as a simple
ASCII stream. The end of the ASCII text stream is indicated by sending a single line consisting of a single period
(".") followed by a carriage return and line feed. Once the
SMTP-Receiver receives the period, it sends a final 250 OK
command to finish the computer-to-computer session.

Notice that the FROM, TO, DATE, SUBJECT, CC, BCC, and other fields in a standard email message are all sent as part of the data and have no special meaning to the SMTP-Sender or SMTP-Receiver. The mail client program, such as Outlook or a Yahoo web mail, extracts the mail addresses from these fields and passes them to the SMTP-Sender.

Over time, mail was used to send a variety of attachments in a variety of formats, from Microsoft Word documents to jpg images. To handle this, a standard was developed called the Multimedia Internet Mail Extensions (MIME) Encoding. MIME is a way for binary data such as Microsoft Word documents or graphic images to be encoded as ASCII text. Once encoded in this way, it can be sent using standard SMTP-Senders and SMTP-Receivers. The same MIME encoding is used today by both SMTP and HTTP.

1.15   The Fourth Era: Clouds of Devices

In the fourth era, hardware cycles and software applications have already become commodities. This era is about the transition from browser-based applications to devices; from copper-based networks to fiber-based and wireless networks; and from an application-based software model to a service-based software model.

The icon of the third era is a PC running a web browser. The problem is that 1990's style PCs were complicated to operate, had to be tethered to networks, and came in basically one style and color. The icon of the fourth era is a wireless pocket device supporting email and instant messaging. The device doesn't need to be booted, simply turned on; it doesn't need a network cable, simply a network; and it doesn't need an operations manual, simply an operator.

In the fourth era, rather than use a single PC running desk top applications in your office, you are more likely to carry several small independent devices, such as email devices, cell phones, music and video players, and games, all connected on wireless IP networks and providing various services. In the same way that a telephone today provides a simple service (you dial a phone number and talk to someone), these devices will also provide equally simple services (you enter an email address, a short note, and push send).

By the end of the fourth era computing devices with embedded wireless networking and general positioning systems (GPS) capabilities will be smaller than postage stamps and cost about the same. They will be included in automobiles to provide early warnings of engine breakdown, attached to bridges to aid in maintenance, and used to keep track of your young children.

In the first two eras, the computer was firmly at the center of the model. Attached to the computer were various peripheral devices, such as terminals, printers and disk drives. In the third era this began to change, with the network moving towards the center. By the fourth era, this transition should be complete, with computer routers and switches firmly at the center of the model, and with CPUs, disk drives, and wireless devices simply peripherals. Sometimes this model is called the "hollowed out computer."

There is no agreed upon name for the fourth era. The fourth era is full of *devices* providing clouds of services over an ever present and ubiquitous IP network. For simplicity, in this book, we will refer to it simply as the Device Era. You should expect this *name* to seem quaint and old fashioned by the time you are reading this book, but I would be surprised if the essence of the era had changed in a significant way.

What is scarce in the fourth era is a way to manage the data and the information produced by the myriad devices and their associated services. The upcoming fifth era is based upon the emerging ability to extract useful information from this data and to structure it in a way that leads to useful decisions.

1.16   Case Study: Routers

This case study is about a piece of hardware called a router that allows two or more computer networks to connect together. The development of the router was one of the critical events that enabled the creation of the Internet.

Viewing a web page on the Internet requires that your computer send messages back and forth with another computer, which is called the web server. In an earlier section, we learned that just as every telephone in the world has a unique phone number, every computer on the Internet has a unique address, called its Internet or IP address.

Very roughly, the Internet, from the network perspective, is a collection of local area networks that are connected together with routers and that communicate with a common set of protocols. These protocols divide data into chunks called packets and attach the IP address of the source and the IP address of the destination to each packet.

As more and more local area networks connected to the Internet, more and more routers were required. The company CISCO was an early supplier of routers. It was founded in 1984. It sold approximately 5,000 routers in 1990 and over 900,000 in 1997. By about 2002, routers could process millions of packets per second, and by 2006, they could process billions of packets per second. Routers contain tables that may have over a hundred thousand entries describing how to route an incoming packet.

Here is how they work in a bit more detail:

Suppose that Computer A in local area network L1 wants to send a message to Computer B on local area network L2. Suppose also that the two local area networks are connected together with a router R having three ports. In this context, a port is a number used to distinguish two or more physical connections of a network to a router. Port P1 is connected to local area network L1, Port P2 is connected to local area network L2, and Port P3 is connected to the local area network of an Internet Service Provider.

Here is what router R does every time it processes a packet.

1. Computer A first breaks the message into units which are each 1500 Bytes long. For simplicity, assume that the message is short and consists of a single 1500 Byte data packet.

2. Given the name of Computer B, Computer A looks up the corresponding IP number for Computer B using a network service called the Domain Name Service or DNS.

3. Computer A then assembles a packet [IP(A), IP(B), data], where IP(A) is the source Internet address of computer A, say a.b.c.d, IP(B) is the destination Internet address of Computer B, say e.f.g.h, and data is the data packet for the message.

4. Computer A looks at the destination address e.f.g.h and determines that it is is not a packet on its own local area network. If it were, the last part of the address would be of the form b.c.d. It therefore sends it to a specific computer called the default gateway, which is specified in the network configuration software of Computer A. Call the default gateway Router R.

5. To send the packet from A to the Router R, the Computer A wraps the IP packet in a frame of the type required by the local area network. For example, if the local area network uses Ethernet, then [MAC(A), MAC(R), IP(A), IP(B), data, CRC]. Here MAC(A) and MAC(R) are the MAC address of the network interfaces for Computer A and Router R on the local area network L1.

6. When Router R gets the packet, it removes the Ethernet Frame to get [IP(A), IP(B), Data]. Router R looks at its router table and finds that IP addresses like B are sent to Port P2 on Router R.

7. To send the packet from Router R to Computer B on local area network L2, Router R places [IP(A), IP(B), Data] into a frame for local area network L2.

8. Computer B on local area network L2 receives the frame, extracts the IP Packet, and then extracts the data.

1.17   The First Half Century of Computing

Study the past if you would define the future.

Confucius

In this section, we broaden our point of view a bit and consider computing *platforms*, which include not only the computer itself, but the broader infrastructure required for computing, including operating systems, applications, storage devices, networks, network services, displays, peripherals, and various other devices that we use when computing.

Viewing computing platforms from the perspective of fifty years or so is difficult for several reasons:

- The different components of a computer and of a computing platform become commoditized at different rates. This is the subject of Chapter 2.

- We are surrounded by marketing clutter and the amount and type of clutter varies from component to component in the computing platform. This is the subject of Chapter 3.

- New technology gets adopted over a period of time. Different factors affect the rate at which different components of a computing platform are adopted. This is the subject of Chapter 4.

In this section, we briefly consider each of the difficulties in turn from the perspective of about fifty years.

Computers vs. Computing Platforms.   As we just mentioned, computers are the most visible component of the computing infrastructure, but not the only component. What we do with computers depends upon the software applications that run on them, the operating systems they employ, the displays and peripherals they use, the networks that connect them, the data that flows through them, and the human-computer interfaces by which we interact with them. One way to to understand the differences between different computing platforms is to answer the following questions:

1. What is the hardware?

2. What is the software?

3. What is the network?

4. What is the user interface?

5. Where is the data?

Table 1.2 summarizes how each computing era has answered these questions differently. It is important to keep two things in mind:

1. First, there is no sharp division between one era and the next. Indeed, it is usually several years into the new era before there is a broad understanding of the nature of the technology of the new era, and a corresponding disappointment in all the utterances by the pundits about the transition.

2. Second, the computing platforms from prior eras never really fade away; instead, they continue to hang around, continue to be used, and continue to evolve. It is simply human nature to focus on what is new.

Scarce and plentiful resources.   A simple means of distinguishing the different computing eras is to ask what component of the computing platform is the bottleneck, and hence is rationed by high prices, and what component is becoming a commodity, characterized by falling prices and rapidly increasing capacity. This is the subject of the second chapter. Table 1.3 provides a high level summary.

Technology adoption.   Despite their name, computers do much more than compute. In fact, relatively few people use them for computing. Today a consumer at home is more likely to use a computer to send email, to buy books, to play games, or to listen to music than to perform a computation. Similarly, a business today is more likely to use a computer to do their accounting, to pay their bills, to manage their inventory, to keep the loyalty of their customers, or to create a marketing brochure.

Each time a new application or function appears, it usually takes much longer than is initially predicted to be adopted. In Chapter 4, we examine some issues that arise and limit the spread of new technology. The term *technology adoption life cycle* is often used to describe the process that limits the spread of new technology. The good news is that you can pay consultants to tell you that the adoption of new technology can be challenging. If you pay them enough, they will tell you that the color of your marketing brochure is wrong and that the tag line you are using in the brochure is not catchy enough. Unfortunately, sometimes the problems are more fundamental.

Question	First Era	Second Era	Third Era	Fourth Era
When?	1965-1985	1980-2000	1995-2015	2005-2025
What is the hardware?	mainframes	servers & PCs	personal computers	devices
What is the software?	back office applications, such as payroll	PC applications, such as word processors and spreadsheets	web applications, such as Amazon and Facebook	services on devices, such as listening to music or taking pictures with cell phones
What is the network?	terminals on serial lines	local area networks	wide area networks	wireless networks
What is the user interface?	terminals	PCs with windows, menus & mice	clicking buttons on browsers	pushing buttons on devices; voice
Where is the data?	in the mainframes	on servers	on desktops	in your pocket

Table 1.2: The first four eras of computing.

	Mainframe Era	PC Era	Web Era	Device Era
What is the bottleneck?	computer cycles	application software	network bandwidth	data
What is becoming commoditized?		computer cycles	application software	network bandwidth

Table 1.3: Viewing the four eras of computing by what is the bottleneck and what is a commodity.

1.18   The Fifth Era: The Commoditization of Data

The majority of books about technology that predict the future age very quickly and become irrelevant within a few years. With this in mind, and with the fifth of era of computing just beginning to emerge, it will be difficult to say very much about it. On the other hand, extrapolating the perspective of the section above, we can provide a rough characterization of some aspects of it:

- Just as the second era commoditized cycles and cylinders, the third era application software, and the fourth era bandwidth, the fifth will commoditize data.

- Once data is commoditized, new types of discovery in science and new types of decision support applications in business will become common.

- The scarce resource in the fifth era of computing will be those individuals with knowledge of how to leverage the technology — everything else will be commoditized or outsourced.

The Fifth Era of Computing will be the subject of Chapter 5. Chapter 5 will discuss the commoditization of data and the emergence of a computing platform that promises to change data-driven decision-making in the same way that during the Fourth Era, the Apple iPod changed how teenagers listened to music.

Chapter 2

Commoditization

2.1 Christmas and Easter

> High-accuracy timekeeping is critical to a number of
> important systems, including telecommunications systems
> that require synchronization to better than 100 billionths
> of a second and satellite navigation systems such as the
> Defense Department's Global Positioning System where
> billionths of a second are significant. Electrical power
> companies use synchronized systems to accurately
> determine the location of faults (for example, lightning
> damage) when they occur and to control the stability of
> their distribution systems. ... Time is also important in
> the ordering of many human activities including the
> activities of financial markets. Time/date stamps are
> used to identify transactions so that these can be placed
> in order, a process that is becoming increasingly
> important as commerce moves electronically at faster and
> faster speeds.

Who Needs High-Accuracy Timekeeping and Why?,
NIST Press Release, December 29, 1999.

Sixty dollars will buy a watch which will keep time to
within a second a year. Periodically, it will connect to an
atomic clock in Boulder, Colorado by radio and synchronize
itself. After ten years, the watch will still be accurate to
within a second. There about 31,556,000 seconds in a year.

The sixty dollar watch will not lose track of any of them. In the words of Dave Barry, I'm not making this up.

Using the watch and a ten dollar calculator, you can calculate the position of the sun and the moon to within a degree two thousand years back in time and two thousand years into the future. This is important, since some holidays, such as Christmas, depend upon the position of the sun, while other holidays, such as Easter, depend upon the position of the moon. Knowing the position of the sun and moon is important, since otherwise you and your family would not know when to get together for holidays, which would be bad.

Five hundred years ago, telling time to within an hour was a challenge and required the best science and technology of the 16th century. Predicting the position of the sun and moon was difficult and astronomical tables could be off by days or even months. Millions of dollars (measured in terms of today's dollars) were spent by the church during the fifteen and sixteenth centuries in order to better calculate the date of Easter. The rules for determining Easter depend upon astronomical tables and getting these tables right was not easy.

During the intervening five hundred years, the accuracy with which we can compute lunar and solar time has increased by about six orders of magnitude, while the cost of instrumentation has decreased from about $10,000,000 to $100 or by a factor of about 100,000. Lawyers can bill in 15 minute increments, doctors can schedule appointments in 7 minute increments, sprinters can win racers by hundredths of a second, and geeks can prefer one computer over another because the clock ticks at 1.2 billion times a second instead of 1.1 billion times a second.

This way of thinking would be incomprehensible to someone in the fifteenth century, yet is understood by any ten year old today. Clearly something has changed. You can view this change as the commoditization of time. Over five hundred years, we can now tell time to an accuracy which is millions of times more accurate and less than a hundred thousandth of the price, and that has changed the way we live our lives.

In this chapter, we will examine the commoditization of several other technologies, some of whose impact is just beginning to be realized.

2.2 Danti's Law: The Commoditization of Time

In the sixteenth century Egnatio Danti wrote a primer on time called the *Sphere of Sacrobosco*. Danti built a meridian, which tracked the progression of sunlight shining through a small hole in a wall using a line (the meridian line) on the floor containing precise markings [73]. Computations based upon meridian measurements were used for calendrical computations, such as measuring accurately the length of the solar year and the length of the lunar month. This was needed since it takes 365.2422 days for the earth to complete its orbit around the sun and 29.53059 days for the moon to complete its orbit around the earth and these numbers are not simple multiples of each other.

A calendar based upon the sun must add corrections so that 0.2422 becomes a whole number. If this is not done accurately, over enough years the seasons will drift with respect to the calendar. This happened to the calendar created by the decree of Julius Caesar in 45 B.C. This calendar worked quite well for a quite a while, but after several centuries needed to be reset. This was finally done by Pope Gregory XIII on October 4, 1582. He decreed the next day to be October 15, 1582 and instituted the calendar that bears his name.

The adoption of new technology is never smooth, something we will discuss in more detail in Chapter 4. Sixteenth century Catholics did not have a problem adopting the Gregorian calendar, but followers of the Church of England did. The British Empire waited until September 2, 1752 to do so, which by decree became September 14, 1752. On that day there were riots in England, but the calendar of the British Empire now agreed with the calendar used by the rest of Europe. Finally, after the October revolution of 1917, Russia also adopted the Gregorian calendar.

Julius Caesar approximated the 365.2422 day solar year by a 365 day year plus an extra 366 day (February 29) every fourth year. This means that Julius Caesar's solar years lasted a bit too long: 365.25 days on average instead of 365.2422 days. Over the decades, Julius Caesar's calendar drifted behind the seasons, causing problems for holidays such as Easter.

Pope Gregory XIII listened to his technology experts and did not count as a leap year any century that was not divisible by 400 as well as 100. For example, 1600 and 2000 are leap years, but 1700, 1800, and 1900 are not. The Gregorian solar years are 365.2425 days on average, better than Julius Caesar's 365.25 days, but still a bit too long.

Even better would be to also not count as a leap year any year divisible by 4000. Call this Kahan's Calendar, after William Kahan of the University of California at Berkeley, someone who has kindly provided open source software to compute dates in this way. With the Gregorian calendar, 2000, 4000, 6000, 8000, 10,000, 12,000 and 14,000 are all leap years. With the Kahan Calendar, only 2000, 6000, 10,000 and 14,000 are leap years. With the Kahan Calendar, the solar year is 365.24225 days on average, which should keep the seasons and the calendar aligned for about 16,000 years. Unfortunately, whether 4,000 is a leap year or not has not been decided. Fortunately, though, there have not yet been any riots about this issue.

Another barrier to the commoditization of time is the difference between the length of a solar day and the length of watch day. A solar day is the length of time between one local noon, where the sun is highest in the sky, and the next. A watch day consists of 24 equal length hours, each consisting of 60 equal length minutes. It is clear that these are quite different — solar days in winter are quite a bit shorter than solar days in summer. One doesn't need a technology expert to see this, simply a five year old who doesn't want to go to bed in the summer because it is still light outside.

There are two factors at work here. First, the rotation of the earth is not perpendicular to the plane of the earth's orbit around the sun (the ecliptic plane). Instead, the axis of the earth's rotation tilts at about 23.5 degrees from the ecliptic plane. To say it another way, the earth rotates obliquely to ecliptic plane. Because of this, the length of the solar day varies from about 8.4 hours to about 16.0 hours, depending upon the day of the year.

Second, because the earth's orbit around the sun is an ellipse and not a circle, its apparent motion is faster at perihelion (around January 2) than at aphelion (around July 3). Because of the obliquity and ellipticity of the earth's orbit, 12 noon in the solar day is up to plus/minus 16 minutes of 12 noon of the watch day. The exact difference is given by the equation of time and can be seen in Figures 2.1 and 2.2. This is important, since for several centuries the only way to accurately set a watch was to use a sun dial and this required corrections using the equation of time. The commoditization of time was not simple, took centuries, and required more spherical trigonometry than is readily available these days, given the wide use of calculators.

2.3   The Commoditization of Space: Harrison's Chronometers

The commoditization of time also ushered along the commoditization of space. Today, we take for granted the wide availability of maps and the ability to accurately determine our latitude and longitude. Using a GPS costing a hundred dollars, we can determine a position to within a dozen yards. Just a few hundred years ago the story was quite different. For example, in the 17th century, trade depended upon ships, and navigating a ship over a trade route required tracking a ship's latitude and longitude. Trade voyages lasted months and being off by a couple of degrees of longitude could easily be the difference between returning safely and not returning at all. When navigating straights, especially when visibility was poor, accurately knowing longitude can be critical. Four minutes of longitude is about 60 miles, which can easily be the difference between sailing safely or running aground. The commoditization of space is another example of a transforming technology which has fundamentally changed our lives.

A ship's latitude could be determined relatively easily by observing the elevation of certain stars over the horizon. On the other hand, determining a ship's longitude required not only astronomical observations, but also knowing the difference between the ship's local solar time and the solar time at a reference point, such as the Greenwich meridian, which is longitude 0. Since there are 360 degrees of longitude and 24 hours in a day, for every 15 degrees (360/24) one travels eastward, the local solar time moves ahead one hour. Solar time means the time as measured by the sun. To determine your longitude, you could use the sun to determine local solar time, compare this to solar time of the Greenwich observatory as maintained by a shipboard chronometer and convert to longitude by using the formula:

longitude in degrees = (local solar time in hours

− Greenwich solar time in hours) · 15 degrees/hour.

For example, determining the longitude to within half a degree on a six week voyage requires a means of maintaining the Greenwich Time to an accuracy of about three seconds a day. Determining time that accurately was possible in the 17th century, but only by using a combination of large pendulum clocks coupled to observatories. These can be thought of as the temporal "mainframes" of the 17th century.

In 1714, the British Parliament offered a reward to "such person or persons as shall discover the Longitude."

The challenge was to determine the longitude on a test voyage from Britain to the West Indies. Twenty thousand pounds was offered for a solution accurate to within half a degree; ten thousand for a solution accurate to within a degree. An Act of Parliament created a Board of Longitude to oversee the trials, to award the prize money, and to ensure that the technology was transferred to the British Navy and the merchant fleet.

Determining time on board a ship in the 18th century was not easy and worked this way: A watch called a marine deck watch was carried to an observatory to be set using the observatory's regulator clock. The deck watch was then returned to the ship where it was used to set the ship's box chronometer, which was rarely moved. The observatory's regulator clock was set using the observatory's transit instrument, which used the position of the sun and stars to set the time.

A watch maker named John Harrison spent most of his life overcoming fundamental engineering challenges to build a chronometer accurate enough to meet the challenge of England's Board of Longitude. The chronometers were called H.1, H.2, H.3, and H.4 (names that would work just as well today for a series of supercomputers) and were built over the period 1730–1761 [129], [67]. England's Navy was important for England's security during this time; and knowing the longitude was critical for Navy ships.

Harrison spent five years designing and building H.1, which weighed about 72 lbs and was about 2 feet by 2 feet by 2 feet in size. H.1 was finished in 1735 and was tested in a voyage from Portsmouth to Lisbon and back.

H.1 was constructed primarily out of wood. It was followed by H.2, which was made out of brass, took another four years, and was even larger, weighing 102 lbs. Harrison then worked on the next design H.3, which took seventeen years to build and was completed in 1757.

Before H.3 was tested at sea, Harrison decided to complete another version, H.4, which was based on the design of the traveling coach clock. H.4 was quite different in appearance than its three earlier siblings and was only 5.2 inches in diameter. H.4 was tested in 1761, when Harrison was sixty seven years old, on a voyage from Portsmouth to Jamaica. It was accurate to within the limits set by the Board of Longitude, but the Board was then strongly influenced by Reverend Nevil Maskelyne, who advocated a different system based using lunar distances to find longitude. Because of this, it was not until 1773 that the Board recognized the success of H.4 by awarding him further funds.

In some sense, things have not changed all that much. The creation of new technology is still dependent upon government funding; the funding is often more closely tied to military applications than most people realize; and personal politics impact the emergence, recognition, and adoption of new technology more than most people would desire.

2.4 Moore's Law: The Commoditization of Processing Power

> The laptop computer I'm using today – an IBM Think Pad with a Pentium III processor – would have ranked as one of the 500 fastest computers in the world in 1995. The exponential growth is just staggering.
>
> Source: Jack Dongarra, Oak Ridge National Laboratory, HPCwire, July 25, 2003, Volume 12, No. 29

The digital era has been fundamentally shaped by the fact that every two to three years it takes about half as long to multiply two numbers using a computer. During this same period the number of transistors that an integrated circuit contains approximately doubles. The hardware providing the processing infrastructure for the digital age is being commoditized, just as the temporal and spatial dimensions were commoditized during the prior 300 hundred years. This commoditization of hardware is usually summarized by citing Moore's Law:

> For more than 30 years, Moore's Law has gov-
> erned Silicon Valley like an immutable force of
> nature. The idea that processing power will
> double every 18 months has been treated as an
> axiom...

From Wired Magazine, May 1997.

Here is how Gordon Moore explains the law named after him:

> Moore's Law is a name that was given to a pro-
> jection I made actually in 1965. I was given the
> chore of predicting what would happen in semi-
> conductor components over the next 10 years
> for the 35th anniversary edition of Electron-
> ics Magazine. That was the early day of in-
> tegrated circuits. The most complicated ones
> on the market had something of the order of 30
> transistors and resistors. We were working on
> things of about twice that complexity, about 60
> components. And I just plotted these on a piece
> of semi long paper and noticed that since the
> first planar transistor was introduced in 1959,
> with integrated circuits following essentially on
> the same technology, that the number of com-
> ponents on an integrated circuit was about dou-
> bling every year.

Source: Moore's Law, An Intel Perspective [94].

Table 2.1 illustrates a remarkable phenomenon. The growth in the computing power of an integrated circuit, as measured by the number of transistors, has grown geometri- cally over a period of roughly thirty five years. At the same time the price per integrated circuit has dropped. It is this phenomenon that we call *commoditization*. More precisely, we say that a technology has been *commoditized* in case, if over a period of years, the following two conditions hold:

1. The function provided by the technology increases geometrically in capacity or capability.

2. Over the same period, the cost of the technology remains the same or decreases.

2.5 Commoditization is All Around Us

The commoditization of digital technology does not end with Moore's Law. What is perhaps surprising is the sheer variety of other digital technologies which have also been commoditized. Not only have integrated circuits been commoditized, but so have disk drives, computer networks, and software. See Table 2.2. Also, as we will describe in detail in Chapter 5, data itself has been commoditized, changing the way we make discoveries.

As we have discussed above, with the emergence of the industrial age, *mechanical devices* commoditized time and space. In some sense, we are in the midst of a second industrial age, in which *digital* devices are taking this commoditization a step further. In this process, the ways we measure time and space have become closely connected. Here are some examples.

In the 1790's, France introduced the metric system to simplify measurements. The meter was define as $1/10,000,000$ the distance between the North Pole and the equator. The problem was that it was not very easy to measure this distance. In 1889, the meter was redefined to be the distance between two lines on a platinum-iridium bar kept at a constant pressure and temperature near Paris. This was better, since it didn't involve getting on a ship, but still not great since there was only one bar at one location. Although the bar could be replicated, this approach allowed lengths to be measured to about one part in a million. This level of accuracy was fine for mechanical devices, but not for digital devices.

Year	Number of Transistors	Processor	Average Yearly Growth	Months to Double
1971	2,300	Intel 4004		
1972	3,500	Intel 8008	52%	20
1974	6,000	Intel 8080	31%	31
1978	29,000	Intel 8086	48%	21
1982	134,000	Intel 286	47%	22
1985	275,000	Intel 386	27%	35
1989	1,200,000	Intel 486	45%	23
1993	3,100,000	Pentium	27%	35
1998	7,500,000	Pentium II	19%	47
2000	28,000,000	Pentium III	93%	13
2003	77,000,000	Pentium IV	40%	25
2006	291,000,000	Intel Core 2 Duo	56%	19

Table 2.1: Over a thirty five year period the number of transistors on an integrated circuit has increased from 2,300 to 291,000,000. This represents geometric growth averaging 44% per year. On average, number of transistors has double every 26 months. For the past several years, Intel has developed several different processors in each product line and the growth rate and doubling period vary a bit depending upon which processors are selected from each product line. Source: The first three columns of data are from the Intel Web site, (www.intel.com). The remaining columns are computed.

Item	Period	Units	Comments
Integrated Circuits	1970 – present	number of transistors per chip	Moore's Law
Storage	1956 – present	Gigabytes per disk	Johnson's Law
Bandwidth	1980 – present	Megabits per second	Gilder's Law
Software	1975 – present	Lines Of Code (LOC) per application or system	Stallman's Law
Data	1975 – present	The number of rows and columns of data in a data set	Bermuda Principles

Table 2.2: This table contains some of the key enabling technologies of the digital era that have been commoditized. The commoditization of processing power has been known as Moore's Law since shortly after it was described by Gordon Moore in 1965. There are no standard names for the commoditization of storage, bandwidth and software. In this book, we refer to the commoditization of storage, bandwidth and software as Johnson's Law, Gilder's Law and Stallman's Law, after Reynold B. Johnson, George Gilder and Richard Stallman, respectively. Perhaps the best example of the the commoditization of data is the availability of the entire human genome, which was provided the Human Genome Project and whose data release policy was governed by what are known as the Bermuda Principles.

In 1960, the meter was redefined as $1,650,763.73$ wavelengths of the reddish-orange light emitted by the rare gas, krypton-86, when heated. This was better since anyone could heat krypton-86, but still provided an accuracy of only about 4 parts per billion.

Things changed in 1983. In that year, again in Paris, the General Conference on Weights and Measures redefined the meter once again. The new definition defined the meter as the distance that light travels in $1/299,792,458$ of a second. Since atomic clocks are accurate to about 1 part in 10^{13}, this in principle improved the accuracy of the meter by at least 10^3. With this definition, length was defined in terms of time.

Although this may seem odd at first, in the digital age of CPUs with clock ticking at over 1 billion times a second and networks that span the earth, this definition is surprisingly natural. For example, three hundred years ago, Chicago and Amsterdam were separated by a five hour difference between local time and Greenwich mean time as measured by a chronometer. Today, they are separated by 110 milliseconds, as measured by the network latency between these two locations.

Network latency is a fundamental property of computer networks. It arises as follows: As we learned in Chapter 1, the most common types of networks today divide data into chunks and put headers on the chunks containing their destination and certain other information to form what are called *packets*. Packets travel over networks at approximately the speed of light. On the other hand, even at this speed, the time required for a packet to travel long distances can begin to add up and affect human computer interactions. This property of packets is called latency.

Latency and bandwidth may appear similar, but in fact are quite different. Think of a long water hose. Latency is the time required for a drop of water to travel from one end of the hose to the other. Bandwidth is the amount of water the hose can deliver per second. A long fire hose has the same latency as a long garden hose, as long as the pressure is the same. On the other hand, the fire hose has much more bandwidth.

The average latency from Chicago to Amsterdam is about 110 milliseconds. The average latency from one side of the Netherlands to the other is about 7 nanoseconds. To summarize, in the digital age, clocks tick at over a billion times a second, distance is naturally measured in terms of these clicks, and we can measure more accurately than ever how late we are.

2.6   The Doubling Game

To understand commoditization, it is helpful to understand a little bit about geometric growth. Geometric growth is easy to understand. With geometric growth, the number of items grows by fixed percentage with each generation, say 25%. In contrast, with arithmetic growth, the number of items grows by a fixed number of items with each generation. After a few generations, the difference is quite striking. See the Table 2.4.

Geometric growth has the following property. If items grow geometrically, then the number of generations required for them to double is constant. In the example above with 25% growth, the number of generations for the items to double is approximately 3.1. Either of these two numbers can be computed from the other. With arithmetic growth the number of generations required for doubling increases with the size of the number. For example, with arithmetic growth it takes four generations for a capacity of two to double to a capacity of four, and eight generations for a capacity of four to double to a capacity of eight. This difference provides a litmus test for commoditization.

If the number of generations required for doubling is constant or decreases, the technology is on the way to being commoditized. If the number of generations required for commoditization increases, then the technology is not yet ready for commoditization. This is the doubling criterion.

Item	Period	Comments
Time	1600-1900	Analog watches keep time to within minutes. They need to be set occasionally using the town's watch tower.
Time	1960-2000	A ten dollar digital watch can determine the time to within a second.
Space	1700-1800	Marine chronometers were developed through advances in mechanics that can determine latitude to within a degree.
Space	1960-2000	A Geographical Positioning System (GPS) can determine position within yards.

Table 2.3: Moore's law describing the commoditization of the processing power of integrated circuits is well known and has occurred over the last 40 years or so. It is useful to apply this perspective to other phenomena, such as the commoditization of how we measure time and space that has occurred over the past few hundred years. During the first industrial era, mechanical devices were developed to measure time and space to an accuracy that was previously unknown. During the second industrial era, digital devices were developed to measure time and space to an accuracy that was previously unknown.

Generation	Geometric	Arithmetic
start	2.00	2.00
1	2.50	2.50
2	3.13	3.00
3	3.91	3.50
4	4.88	4.00
5	6.10	4.50
6	7.63	5.00
7	9.54	5.50
8	11.92	6.00
9	14.90	6.50
10	18.63	7.00
11	23.28	7.50
12	29.10	8.00
13	36.38	8.50
14	45.57	9.00
15	56.84	9.50
16	71.05	10.00
17	88.82	10.50
18	111.02	11.00
19	138.78	11.50
20	173.47	12.00

Table 2.4: This table illustrates the difference between geometric growth and arithmetic growth. The first column contains the generation, the second column the number of items after 25% of geometric growth, and the third column the number of items after adding 0.5 items of arithmetic growth. Note that with each generation, the ratio of geometric growth to arithmetic growth becomes more pronounced. For the first few generations, the ration is about 1; but, after 6 generations, the ratio is over 1.5x; after 9 generations, the ratio is is over 2.0x; and after 18 generations, the ratio is over 10x.

2.7 Transforming Technologies

As we have just discussed, time and space underwent a commoditization during the sixteenth through the eighteenth centuries. The process fundamentally transformed the lives of individuals. During the sixteenth century monks prayed six times a day (at the canonical hours) and a sundial was perfectly adequate for this requirement. Three hundred years later, trains crisscrossed America and this required that the local time be replaced with universal time, that time zones be used so that time could be consistently measured from place to place, and that time be accurately measured to minutes, not hours.

Danti's Law and Moore's Law describe technologies that we call *transforming*. A transforming technology represents a core technological function that has been commoditized and has the following characteristics:

- It is an important enabling technology. In this chapter, we discuss the commoditization of integrated circuits, storage, bandwidth, and software. These are some of the key enabling technologies for today's computing platforms.

- The geometric increase in capacity over decades is not due to a single technology, but rather a number of technologies, most of which were not even invented at the beginning of the phenomenon.

- The phenomenon is *long lived.* Moore's law has persisted for over thirty years, as have similar laws describing the commoditization of bandwidth and software.

- The trend is *regular.* Over thirty years, the average yearly growth has never deviated more than 15 percentage points from the average of 40%.

To summarize, the character of computing, and in particular of Internet computing, is to a large degree determined by transforming technologies that are long lived and regular. These characteristics are in sharp contrast to the way that computing is usually presented as a series of unexpected and revolutionary breakthroughs.

2.8   Storage and Johnson's Law

> Input/output has been the orphan of the computer architecture. Historically neglected by CPU enthusiasts, the prejudice against I/O is institutionalized in the most widely used performance measure, CPU time. ... This attitude is contradicted by common sense. A computer without I/O devices is like a car without wheels – you can't get very far without them.

> John L. Hennessy and David A. Patterson, Computer Architecture: A Quantitative Approach, second edition, Morgan Kaufmann Publishers, Inc., San Francisco, California, 1996, page 485.

The first disk drive was built by a team at IBM headed by Reynold B. Johnson in 1956 for a machine called RAMAC (Random Access Method of Accounting and Control).

The essential design of the disk drive has not changed. The RAMAC disk consisted of fifty platters coated on both sides with a magnetic material. Read/write heads moved over the platters to access information at a specific location.

Data was divided into circular tracks and tracks were divided into sectors by radial lines. Tracks over each other were grouped into cylinders, since the read/write head did not need to move within a cylinder, just to access a different platter. See the Figure 2.1.

The RAMAC disk consisted of fifty aluminum platters coated with iron oxide. The disks were two feet in diameter and used two read/write heads. They rotated at 1,200 rpm. Each side of the disk had 100 tracks, each of which could hold 500 characters. The entire disk could hold about 5 MB of data.

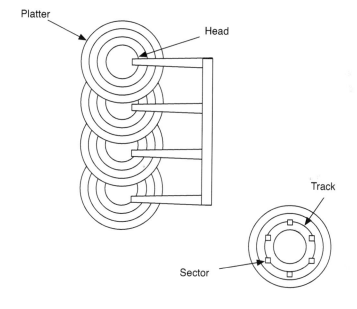

Figure 2.1: The basic design of a disk drive has not changed since the first disk drive built in 1956. Disks are divided into platters, platters into tracks, and tracks into sectors.

By 2007, you could buy a disk from Amazon for $400 that stores 750 GB of data, consisting of 4 platters that rotate at 7,200 rpm. During the period 1956–2007, the surface area of a disk has shrunk by a factor of about 800, while the storage capacity has increased by about 150,000 times. This means that the number of bits stored by square inch (the areal density) has increased by a factor of about 120 million.

During the period 1960–1990, the areal density doubled about every three years. In 1991, a new technology for read heads called magneto-resistive (MR) read heads reduced the doubling time to about two years.

Over this period, the cost of storing a megabyte of data has fallen from about $10,000 in 1956, to about $100 in the early 1980's, to about $1 in the mid 1990's. In 2002, the cost was about $1 per gigabyte, much less than the cost of paper required to store the same amount of information [57]. Five years later, in 2007, the cost for a gigabyte of storage was about $0.53. In other words, over a period of about 50 years, the cost to store a gigabyte of data has fallen from $10,000,000 to just over 50 cents.

To summarize, data storage has become commoditized and is just as much a transforming technology as CPU cycles. Data storage is often used in surprising ways. Napster, which operated between June 1999 and July 2000, exploited the fact that student dormitories contained lots of unused gigabytes to create a distributed storage and access system that contained millions of disk drives. At one point Napster had over ten million users. If we assume that each user provided approximate 100 megabytes of storage to Napster, then the Napster network had an aggregate distributed storage of 1000 terabytes or 1 petabyte. This means that a student in a dormitory in 2000 could access over 100 million times as much on line disk storage as a scientist or engineer could in 1960.

Year	Size (GB)	Brand	Average Yearly Growth	Months to Double
1980	0.005	Seagate Technology ST506 5.25 inch		
1983	0.01	Rodime RO 352 3.5 inch	26%	36
1988	0.02	PrairieTech 220 2.5 inch	15%	60
1991	0.04	Maxtor 7000 Series 3524	26%	36
1993	2.1	Seagate Technology ST12550 Barracuda	625%	4
2001	80	Seagate Technology Barracuda IV	58%	18
2002	120	Seagate Technology Barracuda V	50%	21
2006	750	Seagate Technology Barracuda 7200.10	58%	18

Table 2.5: Over the past 25 years, disks that are small enough to fit into a personal computer have grown by a factor of about 150,000x, from 5 MB to 750,000 MB.

2.9   Bandwidth and Gilder's Law

The bandwidth of optical fibers doubles every six months.

Gilder's Law - various sources.

Beginning with an influential 1993 Forbes ASAP article, George Gilder popularized two fundamental insights that are complementary, and mutually reinforcing.

1. The *price* of bandwidth is being commoditized (Gilder's Law).

2. The *value* of a network increases as the square of the number of nodes (Metcalfe's Law).

Gilder's influence was based not just on his insight into these two phenomena, but also, at least in part, to the prophetic quality of his pronouncements. He compared and contrasted the *microcosm* created by the commoditization of microprocessors to the *telecosm* created by the commoditization of bandwidth.

Here is an example:

> Meanwhile, the law of the telecosm is launching a similar spiral of performance in transmission media, ultimately increasing their bandwidth, also by a factor of millions. Bandwidth is a replacement for switches. If you can put enough detailed addressing, routing, prioritization and other information on the packets, you don't have to worry about channeling the data through ATM switches. The emergence of dumb, passive all-optical networks with bandwidths some ten-thousandfold larger than existing fiber optics will obviate much of the pressure on switches.
>
> George Gilder, Metcalfe's Law and Legacy, Forbes ASAP, September 13, 1993.

Roughly speaking, the Internet can be thought of as millions of nodes that can communicate with each other by passing messages over a network of networks. The maximum speed of these networks has grown geometrically over the past twenty years or so, from 56 Kb/s in 1986 to over 1 Gb/s in 2001. By 2007, 10 Gb/s networks were being deployed and by 2010 100 Gb/s networks were being deployed.n

Roughly speaking the Internet as a *communications* network has approximately the same complexity and cost as the telephone network. On the other hand, the two are organized quite differently. The telephone network consists of a smart network with relatively dumb user devices (telephones), while the Internet consists of a dumb network using packet switching, with relatively smart user devices (computers).

2.10   Software and Stallman's Law

Once GNU is written, everyone will be able to obtain good system software free, just like air.

Richard Stallman, The GNU Manifesto, 1985.

Richard Stallman is a software developer who, beginning about 1984, articulated a vision for software in which it is just as much a commodity as air. Remarkably, in less than twenty years, this vision became a reality.

Operating systems are expensive to build and maintain. As a very rough order of magnitude estimate, it requires about $10,000,000 per year of engineering costs to develop and maintain an operating system. Here are two examples: Ten million dollars is the amount of revenue generated if 1,000,000 users pay Microsoft about $100 for each license of Microsoft's Windows. Ten million dollars is also the amount of revenue generated if 100,000 users pay $1,000 to Sun Microsystems for Sun's Solaris. With these user

Year	Mbps	AYG (%)	Months to Double	Comments
1986	0.056			NSFNET started
1988	1.544	425	5	NSFNET backbone upgraded to T1
1991	44.736	207	7	NSFNET backbone upgraded to T3
1995	155.52	37	27	vBNS started with OC-3 backbone
1997	622.08	100	12	vBNS backbone upgraded OC-12
1999	2,500	100	12	vBNS backbone upgraded OC-48
2001	10,000	100	12	MREN backbone operates at 10GE
2006	40,000	32	30	Some limited deployment in Japan of OC-768

Table 2.6: Data about Gilder's law is a bit harder to get than data about Moore's Law. To quantify the growth in bandwidth over a fifteen year period, this table details the bandwidth of the backbone of some academic research network during the twenty year period 1986–2006. During this period, the average yearly growth (AYG) has been about 143%, while the average time to double has been about 15 months. Note that Gilder's Law is a bit more optimistic.

bases, both companies can produce operating systems and be profitable.

This back of the envelope rule is sometimes called *Bill's Law*. The Bill in Bill's Law refers to both to Bill Gates, the co-founder and Chief Software Architect of Microsoft, and Bill Joy, the co-founder and Chief Scientist of Sun Microsystems. Bill Gates' Rule: "Don't write software for less than 1,000,000 platforms." Bill Joy's Rule: "Don't write software for less than 100,000 platforms."

Actually, during the past few years, Bill's Law has become a bit more complicated: In 2005, Sun Microsystems began a transition that transformed Solaris into an open source operating system. Clients can elect to pay Sun for support and maintenance contracts. In the same year, Microsoft's Client business segment, which included Microsoft's Windows XP, as well as Microsoft's other operating systems, generated $12.1 Billion of revenue or over a thousand times the $10 million estimate above, but you get the idea — it is expensive to develop an operating system.

Because of the cost and complexity, relatively few companies have developed operating systems, and even fewer have survived and evolved for a decade or more. Successful operating systems include Microsoft's DOS, Windows NT, and Windows XP; IBM's MVS; Sun's Solaris; and Apple's Mac OS. Bill's Law was perceived as a barrier to the commoditization of operating systems and the lack of commoditization of operating systems was perceived as a barrier to the commoditization of software.

Linux changed all that. The Linux operating system is developed and maintained by volunteers, but has approximately the same user base as Sun's Solaris. The Linux operating system itself is free if downloaded over the net, but a number of third party vendors, such as RedHat, distribute Linux and provide support and maintenance. That a operating system could be developed and maintained by a loosely organized group of volunteers was unexpected and was the result of a number of different factors that emerged over a period of several decades. For example, the infrastructure for the thousands of volunteers to work together on the Linux distribution depends upon email and web based collaboration software. Without these types of tools, it is very hard to imagine how so many distributed volunteers could work together on so complex a project.

Using a commonly employed measure of the cost to develop software called the COCOMO cost model, it would take over 8,000 person years of development and over one billion dollars to develop the 30,000,000 lines of source code in the 7.1 Release of RedHat. As members of the U.S. Congress are prone to say, a billion here and a billion there add up to real money.

The term *open source* itself is more recent, dating from a meeting in April, 1998 hosted by Tim O'Reiley [119]. The term was adopted to shed some of the baggage associated with the previous term *free software*, which had negative connotations to many business users at that time, such as unreliable, unsupported, not commercial quality, etc.

One of the key events in the commoditization of software occurred over 20 years ago when Richard Stallman started the GNU project in 1984. At the beginning of the GNU project, Stallman wrote a manifesto explaining the project and why he was undertaking it.

> I consider that the golden rule requires that if I like a program I must share it with other people who like it. Software sellers want to divide the users and conquer them, making each user agree not to share with others. I refuse to break solidarity with other users in this way. I cannot in good conscience sign a nondisclosure agreement or a software license agreement. For years I worked within the Artificial Intelligence Lab to resist such tendencies and other inhospitalities, but eventually they had gone too far: I could not remain in an institution where such things are done for me against my will.
>
> Richard Stallman, The GNU Manifesto, 1985.

Product	SLOC
NASA Space Shuttle flight control	420K (shuttle); 1.4 million (ground)
Sun Solaris (1998-2000)	7-8 million
Microsoft Windows 3.1 (1992)	3 million
Microsoft Windows 95	15 million
Microsoft Windows 98	18 million
Microsoft Windows NT 5.0 (1998)	20 million
Microsoft 2000 (2000)	29 million
Microsoft XP (2001)	40 million
Red Hat Linux 6.2 (2000)	17 million
Red Hat Linux 7.1 (2001)	30 million
Red Hat Linux 8.0 (2002)	50 million
Debian 2.2 (2001)	55 million
Debian 3.0 (2002)	105 million
Debian 3.1 (2005)	230 million

Table 2.7: Software has become commoditized. The NASA Space Shuttle code was less than 2 million SLOC and took cost about $100 million dollars per year to develop. Linux contains tens of million of lines of source code and is available for free. Sources: [157], [98], and [4].

GNU began with just a few programs targeted at software engineers: a text editor called Emacs, a debugger to help programmers find software bugs, a parser and a linker, which are tools for programmers and about 35 utilities or small programs.

It turns out that because of the way the industry works and because of the way software licenses work, for software to be free, it must be licensed. To keep software free, Stallman developed a software license to ensure that there would be no restrictions on any application which included GNU software. This license eventually became known by its initials (GPL): The idea of the license is simple:

> GNU is not in the public domain. Everyone will be permitted to modify and redistribute GNU, but no distributor will be allowed to restrict its further redistribution. That is to say, proprietary modifications will not be allowed. I want to make sure that all versions of GNU remain free.

> Richard Stallman, The GNU Manifesto, 1985.

Software applications are often complex, consisting of many different components, written by many different software engineers, from many different organizations. Restrictions on any single component, no matter how small, affect the entire application, since the application cannot run without the component, at least without some modification. The GNU license was viral in the sense that any software distributed with any GNU software as a component had to carry the GNU license. This turned out to work well and to lay the foundation for today's open source software. Over time though, it became clear that this approach to licensing was too restrictive for some applications and several other open source software licenses began to be used. [49].

Many open source projects succeed despite the fact that they ignore many of the basic principles of good software

Year	Version	Estimated SLOC	AYG	Months to Double
1991	0.01	10,000		
1992	0.96	40,000	300%	6
1993	0.99	100,000	150%	9
1994	1.0	170,000	70%	16
1995	1.2	250,000	47%	22
1996	2.0	400,000	60%	18
1997	2.1	800,000	100%	12
1998	2.1.110	1,500,000	88%	13
2000	RedHat 6.2	1,500,000; 17,000,000	237%	7
2001	RedHat 7.1	2,400,000; 30,000,000	76%	15

Table 2.8: The commoditization of software as illustrated by Linux. Linux is a volunteer effort. Prior to the success of Linux, according to conventional wisdom, it was not practical for a collection of individuals to develop an operating system — that was something that could only be done by companies such as Microsoft, IBM, Sun and Apple. SLOC is an abbreviation for source lines of code. AYG is an abbreviation for average yearly growth. The two numbers for the RedHat 6.2 and 7.1 refer to the estimated number of lines in the Linux kernel and the Linux distribution. Using a commonly employed measure of the cost to develop software called the COCOMO cost model, it would take over 8,000 person years of development and over one billion dollars to develop the 30,000,000 lines of source code in the 7.1 Release of RedHat. Sources: [86], [156], and [157].

engineering. Developing good software is extremely difficult. The goal of software engineering is to a provide a framework of techniques so that software projects are more likely to succeed. Although there are quite a few different software engineering methodologies, most are based on the following fundamental observation: If a software project is divided into three phases, design, coding, and testing, then approximately equal time should be spent with each. In contrast, the natural inclination of software engineers is to spend all the time coding — this is the fun part — and to leave to others the design and testing.

In some very rough sense, vendor developed software has the advantage with the first phase (design), while open source software projects have a potential advantage with the second two phases (coding and testing). Successful open source projects have usually had one or a handful of key volunteer developers who created the overall design and coded the *key* components, and then leverage the open source community to flesh out the development and to undertake the testing.

Today, Source Forge, one of the open source software development platforms, has over 50,000 registered open source software projects. Most will never be used. On the other hand, by a process not all that different from software Darwinism, a handful will be widely successful. Of the latter, although they usually do not start with a good design, a good design is almost always a part of the project by the second or third versions.

The third era of computing was an era in which software was a gating factor. With the arrival of the fourth era and the emergence of many successful open source software projects, software is now a commodity.

2.11   Data and the Bermuda Principles

The amount of data available on the Internet is growing geometrically. This is one of the drivers for the Fifth Era of computing that will emerge over the next decade or so and is discussed in more detail in Chapter 5.

As a motivating example, Table 2.9 describes the growth during the past two decades of genetic sequence data in GenBank, which is maintained by the U.S. National Institute of Health (NIH). GenBank was created as part of the Human Genome Project (1990–2003). The goals of the Human Genome Project included i) determining the sequences of the 3 billion chemical base pairs (G, T, C and A) that make up human DNA; ii) identifying the approximately 20,000 - 25,000 genes in human DNA; and iii) storing the information in a database (which became GenBank). Here is an example of the base pairs that make up one of our genes:

```
gagccccagg actgagatat ttttactata ccttctctat
```

One of the reasons that GenBank had such an important impact is that the data it contains is freely available. The release of data in the Human Genome Project is governed by what are sometimes called the Bermuda Principles. The Bermuda Principles calls explicitly for the rapid public release of DNA sequence data. Think of this as an example of open data, broadly analogous to open source software. Open data promises to be just as much as a transforming technology as open source software, although its impact may be further out.

GenBank is just one example of the open data that is available on the web. The number of data sources like GenBank available over the web has not been accurately measured. As a very rough estimate, if just 0.1% of the web sites on the Internet made available some open data, then there would be over 250,000 sources of open data.

2.12   Network Effects

Ethernet works in practice but not in theory.

Attributed to Robert Metcalfe

Year	Base Pairs	Sequences	AYG	Months to Double
1982	680338	606		
1983	2274029	2427	234%	7
1984	3368765	4175	48%	21
1985	5204420	5700	54%	19
1986	9615371	9978	85%	14
1987	15514776	14584	61%	17
1988	23800000	20579	53%	19
1989	34762585	28791	46%	22
1990	49179285	39533	41%	24
1991	71947426	55627	46%	22
1992	101008486	78608	40%	25
1993	157152442	143492	56%	19
1994	217102462	215273	38%	26
1995	384939485	555694	77%	15
1996	651972984	1021211	69%	16
1997	1160300687	1765847	78%	14
1998	2008761784	2837897	73%	15
1999	3841163011	4864570	91%	13
2000	11101066288	10106023	189%	8
2001	15849921438	14976310	43%	23
2002	28507990166	22318883	80%	14
2003	36553368485	30968418	28%	33
2004	44575745176	40604319	22%	42
2005	56037734462	52016762	26%	36
2006	59750386305	54584635	7%	130
2007	71292211453	67218344	19%	47

Table 2.9: The amount of sequence data in GenBank has grown exponentially during the past twenty five years. Over this period the average annual growth in sequence data has been about 64% and the average doubling period has about 25.6 months.

We have already examined Gilder's Law that describes the commoditization of bandwidth. Gilder was one of the first to popularize what he called the network effects of communications networks. Here is how he described it:

> In this era of networking, [Robert Metcalfe] is the author of what I will call Metcalfe's law of the telecosm, showing the magic of interconnections: connect any number, "n," of machines — whether computers, phones or even cars — and you get "n" squared potential value. Think of phones without networks or cars without roads. Conversely, imagine the benefits of linking up tens of millions of computers and sense the exponential power of the telecosm.
>
> George Gilder, Metcalfe's Law and Legacy, Forbes ASAP, September 13, 1993. Also, George Gilder, Telecosm, Simon and Schuster, 1996.

Metcalfe's Law is based upon the observation that given a network with n nodes, each node can communicate with up to $n - 1$ other nodes, and so there $\frac{1}{2}n(n - 1)$ different communications paths in the network. For large n, this is approximately n^2. If the value of each new link is a constant, then the value of a network of n nodes grows as n^2.

Unlike Gilder's Law about the commoditization of bandwidth, which is more or less a direct consequence of the falling price and increasing power of devices such as network routers and switches, Metcalfe's Law is an observation about the *structural* properties of large networks. There is an important difference between Gilder's Law and Metcalfe's Law: The amount of available bandwidth and its cost can, in principle, be computed each year. In contrast, the *value* of a network node, is usually much harder to measure. For this reason, although it seems consistent with experience that the value of a network increases with the number of nodes n, there is no consensus at this time how best to measure the value of a node in a network and whether the value of a network increases like n, or $n \log n$, or n^2, or in some other way.

Network effects arise, in part, when one product or service has a small advantage over another, and through a feedback mechanism, that advantage begins to grow. This is sometimes called a feedback loop, after the feedback displayed by electrical circuits and control systems. Here is how Bill Gates describes the feedback loop, which he feels was partly responsible for the creation of the Microsoft monopoly:

> A positive-feedback cycle begins when, in a growing market, one way of doing something gets a slight advantage over its competitors. It is most likely to happen with high-technology products that can be made in great volume for very little increase in cost and derive some of their value from their compatibility. ... A positive-feedback cycle began driving the PC market. Once it got going, thousands of software applications appeared, and untold numbers of companies began making add-in or "accessory" cards, which extended the hardware capabilities of the PC.
>
> Bill Gates, The Road Ahead.

Over the past several years, economists have become interested in network effects, especially network effects in technology markets. This is good, since this provides some hope that careful measurements about network effects may be done in the future. Here is a list of some of the mechanisms that are beginning to be associated with network effects in a technology market: lock-in to particular technology standards; high inertia for established standards and high volatility for immature standards; intense competition in the early market, followed by scant competition in the mature market; and first mover advantages, followed by

	CPUs	Bandwidth	Software	Data
Devices or Instance Level	Moore's Law	Gilder's Law	Stallman's Law	Bermuda Principles
Network Level	Grids	Metcalfe's Law	Linus's Law	Pearson's Law

Table 2.10: As components become commoditized, their numbers increase and network effects become apparent.

barriers to entry. These characteristics explain, in part, the rocky road many good technologies have in the market, and the longevity of many poor technologies. We return to this subject in Chapter 4.

Each of the commoditized technologies described in this chapter have a corresponding network effect. See Table 2.10. For example, the emergence of global grids of computers can be thought of as the corresponding network effect for Moore's Law for processors, in the same way that Metcalfe's Law is the corresponding network effect of Gilder's Law for bandwidth. The network effects corresponding to software and data are just beginning to emerge. We will consider network effects associated with data briefly in Chapter 5.

Chapter 3

Technical Innovation vs. Market Clutter

3.1 Technical Innovation vs. Market Clutter

> Each generation has its few great mathematicians, and mathematics would not even notice the absence of the others. They are useful as teachers, and their research harms no one, but it is of no importance at all. A mathematician is great or he is nothing. ... The mathematical life of a mathematician is short. Work rarely improves after the age of twenty-five or thirty. If little has been accomplished by then, little will ever be accomplished.

Alfred Adler, Mathematics and Creativity, 1972 [2]

> Hollywood has its Oscars. Television has its Emmys. Broadway has its Tonys. And advertising has its Clios. And its Andys, Addys, Effies and Obies. And 117 other assorted awards. And those are just the big ones.

Joanne Lipman, 1987 [41]

In this chapter, we examine the second and third themes of this book—the rarity of innovation and the pervasiveness

81

of market clutter. The consensus of most experts in a field is that technical innovation is relatively rare in the sense that genuinely novel ideas occur only every few years. A consequence of this is that by beginning with a firm foundation of the basic principles in a field and by keeping up with the genuine innovations, it is practical to have a good, if not detailed, understanding of a technical field.

On the other hand, reading almost any business or computer industry publication generally produces the opposite impression — that many companies are innovative and that only by working with these innovative companies can you keep up. In other words, the market is cluttered by companies claiming to be innovative and claiming to offer products and services that they assert are essential if you want to remain productive and competitive.

There is a fundamental tension between the actual pace of technical innovation and claims made in the market place, most of which just add to the clutter. For this reason, making technological decisions and completing technical projects is quite challenging.

In this chapter, we begin by looking at technical innovation in greater detail. Broadly speaking, the power of a computer today can be measured along several different axes: how fast it can compute, how much it can store, and how many other computers it can communicate with. For this reason, we look at three case studies in innovation: one that is related to computation involving prime numbers; one that is related to storage, the evolution of the database; and one that is related to communication, routing packets.

We then look at some of the reasons for market clutter, not all of which are pretty. One reason for clutter is that everyone likes to work with winners. The result is instead of a market of 60 technology vendors selling database software with three winners and 57 non-winners, there are 20 sub-markets consisting of three winners each, plus full employment for a large number of marketing consultants whose job is to create and maintain these 20 sub-markets.

3.2 A Case Study in Innovation: Approximating Solutions to Equations

This case study is about an innovation in computing that dates back to the 17th century but is still commonly used. The innovation was a new way to approximate solutions to equations and was introduced by Isaac Newton.

A good way to describe the method Newton introduced is to show how it applies to finding square roots, which can be thought of as the solution of an equation involving the square of a variable, such as x. Square roots are naturally associated with right triangles, which is where we begin.

About 530 BC, Pythagoras knew that if a right triangle has sides of length a, b and c, then (using modern language), the square of the longest side (call it c) is the sum of the squares of the other two sides (a and b). The simplest case is when $a = b = 1$, and, in this case, computing c is the same thing as computing the square root of 2.

Pythagoras discovered that c cannot be written as a fraction a/b, where a and b are integers. This was probably one of the first numbers discovered that one could be sure could not be written as a fraction of two integers. The notes for this chapter contain a simple argument why this is so.

To understand innovation in computation generally, it is instructive to understand Newton's method in more detail.

The Pythagoreans viewed numbers from a geometric point of view in the sense that integers were often viewed as lengths — think of a ruler with n equally spaced tick marks, one for each integer being counted. A compass could be used to create the tick marks on the ruler, and the ruler and compass together could be used to construct triangles and other geometric objects, as is taught in a high school geometry course.

From this viewpoint, fractions such as a/b, arise naturally with triangles when you consider the ratio of two sides of a triangle or rectangle. It was reasonable to assume that if the distance between the tick marks was made small enough, then any number that arises from a construction using a ruler and a compass could be written this way.

It turns out that this is not the case. It was this fact that the Pythagoreans discovered and which caused so much angst.

Today, we are familiar with lots of numbers that cannot be expressed as integers or ratios of integers, but for Pythagoras and members of his school this was a very important discovery, and one that probably caused a fair amount of discomfort, for the simple reason that it must have seen very odd that such a simple triangle (a right triangle with two sides the same length) did not fit into their framework.

On the other hand, to understand numbers such as c above, a different point of view is required. Rather than think of numbers as counting objects, or as geometric lengths and ratios of lengths, numbers can be thought of as the solutions to certain types of equations. One of the simplest such equations is the equation that the square of c is the sum of the squares of a and b. Although, this is a familiar point of view for us today, it was not so for the Greeks in Pythagoras' time.

If numbers are thought of from this point of view, here is a natural question to ask: Given an equation, how can you find the numbers that solve the equation? It turns out that this is a difficult problem. One of the most powerful algorithms for solving equations was discovered and refined by several mathematicians in the 17th century, including Newton.

During the period 1664 – 1671, Newton discovered a simple way to approximate solutions to a very wide class of equations. Newton's method is an iterative algorithm, which, given a guess, say x_n that is close to the answer, refines the guess with a new guess x_{n+1} that is even closer to the answer. In other words, rather than trying write down the solution using a formula (which is usually quite difficult to do) an iterative algorithm begins with a guess x_0 and produces a sequence

$$x_0, x_1, x_2, x_3, \ldots$$

that get closer and closer to the solution of the equation.

The version of the algorithm that is usually used today is due to Raphson, who published a version in 1697. To illustrate this, here is how, what is today called the Newton-Raphson Method, can be used to find the square root of a number c:

1. Begin with a very estimate (a guess) for the square root of c, say $x_0 = 1$.

2. Compute $x_{n+1} = x_n - (x_n^2 - c)/2x_n$, for $n \geq 1$.

3. If x_{n+1} and x_n are close together, stop because you have found an approximation to the square root c. If not, return to Step 2, to compute the next iteration in the sequence.

Note that this algorithm, estimates x_1 from the initial guess x_0; estimates x_2 from the estimate x_1; estimates x_3 from the estimate x_2, etc. We can write a Python program to compute $x_1, x_2, \ldots, x_n$ in a few lines:

```
def sqrt(c,n):
    x = 1.0
    for i in range(1,n):
        x = x - (x*x-c)/(2*x)
    return x
```

If this were part of a real computer program, we would have to be more careful and check to see if x is close to zero so we don't divide by zero and to check more carefully when to stop. On the other hand, for our purposes here, these five lines are all we need, and this is what we find:

Iterative methods like the Newton-Raphson method have turned out to be a major innovation: not only does the algorithm efficiently find square roots, but it also can find the solution to a wide variety of different types of equations.

Iteration	Sqrt 2	Check
1	1.0	1.0
2	1.5	2.25
3	1.41666666667	2.00694444444
4	1.41421568627	2.0000060073
5	1.41421356237	2.0
6	1.41421356237	2.0
7	1.41421356237	2.0

Iteration	Sqrt 3	Check
1	1.0	1.0
2	2.0	4.0
3	1.75	3.0625
4	1.73214285714	3.00031887755
5	1.73205081001	3.00000000847
6	1.73205080757	3.0
7	1.73205080757	3.0

Iteration	Sqrt 5	Check
1	1.0	1.0
2	3.0	9.0
3	2.33333333333	5.44444444444
4	2.2380952381	5.00907029478
5	2.23606889564	5.00000410606
6	2.2360679775	5.0
7	2.2360679775	5.0

Table 3.1: Computing square roots using the Newton-Raphson Method contained in the program fragment above.

The Newton-Raphson method also gave us new ways to think of numbers. Recall that prior to algorithms like this, numbers were thought of as representing counts, ratios of counts, lengths, and ratios of lengths. With the Newton-Raphson method, it also becomes natural to think of numbers as being the solutions of equations and as the limits of iterations.

3.3   A Case Study in Clutter: Business Intelligence

In the last section, we presented a case study in innovation. In this section, we consider the other extreme and present a short case study in market clutter.

Data mining is a relatively new field that began in the early 1990's, although the roots are older. The goal of data mining is to find interesting structures in data. As the amount of digital data grew, traditional statistical techniques did not always scale to large data sets and a variety of new techniques were developed, and are still being developed, to address this requirement. From this perspective, data mining can be thought of as *statistics on steroids,* where steroids in this context is a metaphor for high performance computers.

Each year there are several technical conferences in the field that have papers describing data mining techniques and their applications. One of the oldest is the ACM SIGKDD International Conference on Knowledge Discovery and Data Mining, which began in 1995.

I was the general chair for the 11th SIGKDD conference that took place in Chicago during August, 2005 (KDD 2005). One of my tasks was to be part of a technical committee that selected some of the most influential papers that were published in the field during the previous 10 years. Each year since 1995, the ACM SIGKDD conference has published about 50–100 papers. After looking at the resulting list of several hundred papers, it was clear that field had produced some important advances, but it was equally clear that many of the papers were not as significant several years later as they might have seemed at the time.

Sitting down with the spreadsheet listing the paper titles and authors and looking back over the ten years, it was easy to be proud of the field's accomplishments.

On the other hand, at about the same time that the KDD 2005 took place, the phrase "data mining" returned about 7,790,000 results and 48 sponsored links on Google; 11,000,000 documents and 11 sponsored links on Yahoo; and 3,000,000 documents and 8 sponsored links on MSN Search. The most charitable description I have for most of these documents is that they are simply clutter. The clutter produced by this many documents can also lead to despair, or what Richard Saul Wurman describes as *information anxiety* [160].

When data mining technology is used to analyze business data, the term *business intelligence* is usually used. In 2005, phrase "business intelligence" returned 17,900,000 results and 48 sponsored links on Google; 28,000,000 results and 11 sponsored links on Yahoo; and 6,700,000 results and 8 sponsored links on MSN Search. The number of results returned grows each day and represents a lot of clutter.

There is general consensus in the business intelligence field today about the main steps required when undertaking a business intelligence project, and in the data mining field, about the main innovations in the field that have taken place over the past decade. The problem is that it is difficult to identify what is essential, given all the clutter produced by these millions of documents.

3.4   The Changing Perception of Technical Innovation

The perception of what is innovative almost always changes over time. Agreement about what is innovative seems to go through phases, with each phase taking approximately a decade or so:

1. *Chaos.* The first phase is one of chaos without any agreement on what is innovative. The only people claiming to know are the pundits, and they are almost always wrong during this period.

2. *Consensus.* In the second phase, a consensus emerges and most of the experts agree on what is innovative. This is the nicest phase since it is rare for experts to agree.

3. *Simplification.* In the third phase, the views of the researchers in the field are simplified, pared down and become more broadly known. Most popular accounts tend to describe the field using essentially the same terms and simplifications.

4. *Revision.* In the fourth phase, historians begin to look at the events in some detail and with some historical perspective. During this phase, the consensus view sometimes changes. On the other hand, no one seems to care much.

To better understand these phases, let us examine some of the computing infrastructure underlying the web from this perspective.

Chaos. In this phase, experts in the field tend to view their own work as innovative, but under-appreciated, while outsiders tend to have quite varied and idiosyncratic views about what is innovative. Today, the field of distributed computing is in a chaotic period. The claims for innovations include peer-to-peer computing, cloud computing, service-based architectures, collaborative computing, etc.

Consensus. After a decade or so, a consensus slowly begins to emerge. Most experts in the field tend to agree on the key events and their significance. Outsiders tend to be aware of the key events, but do not always fully understand them. Several papers have come to be viewed as pivotal.

Journalists have written anecdotal histories. For example, there is a broad consensus about the early history of the Internet today, with the following key events usually being included [102] :

- 1962 - Leonard Kleinrock invents packet-switching technology.

- 1963 - J.C.R. Licklider, head of computer research at ARPA, articulates vision of worldwide network.

- 1967 - Larry Roberts publishes a paper proposing the ARPAnet network.

- 1968 - DOD initiates the ARPAnet development.

- 1972 - E-mail introduced by Ray Tomlinson.

- 1989 - Tim Berners-Lee introduces the world wide web

- 1991 - Gopher, a document retrieval system, is introduced at University of Minnesota

- 1993 - Marc Andreesen develops MOSAIC, the first Internet browser, at the University of Illinois

Simplification.   After another decade or so, the consensus view tends to become simpler and more pared down. For example, here is a description from Business Week in 2000 of a description of the history of the web: "In 1989, Tim Berners-Lee, a researcher at CERN, the high-energy physics laboratory in Geneva, Switzerland, invented a way to link together documents on research projects so they could be accessed over computer networks. He called it the World Wide Web [74]." The chronology above is now simplified to:

- 1989 - Tim Berners-Lee invents the web

- 1993 - Marc Andreesen develops MOSAIC, the first Internet browser, at the University of Illinois

Revision. Since the web is a bit young for a revisionist history, consider the early history of the computer, which is currently going through a revisionist period. One of the key events was the publication in 1945 of the EDVAC Report written by John von Neumann. John von Neumann (1903–1957) made fundamental contributions in mathematics as well as several other fields and the EDVAC Report was widely circulated and influential. A number of scientists, including Aiken, Atanasoff, Eckert and Mauchly, also made key contributions at that time. These contributions tended to be forgotten and overshadowed by von Neumann's contribution during the phase in which the history became simplified. The early history of the computer is now being sorted out and several revisionist histories have been written, including the popular book *ENIAC* by Scott McKartney [85]. In these revisionist histories, some of the contributions that were forgotten for a time are being highlighted again.

3.5   The Imperative to be in the Upper Right

People like winners. Most of us can remember the first person to step on the moon, but few of us can remember the second person to step on the moon. There are over 600 publicly traded software companies and not all of them can be number 1. This creates a problem for software companies that naturally enough want to be remembered as number 1, and one of the principal goals of marketing is to try in some way to make their company a leader. This creates lots of market clutter.

There are several standard things that companies do in order to position themselves as a leader.

Introduce a sub-market. A good strategy is for a vendor

to introduce a sub-market and to define the sub-market in such a way that they are number one. For example, in 2001 within data warehousing, Cognos was the leader of ad hoc querying, Microstrategy was the leader of server side OLAP, Business Objects was the leader of client side object, Crystal Reports was the leader of end user reporting, and SAS was the leader of decision support systems. A couple of years earlier and a couple of years later, there were different sub-markets, which only added to the clutter.

Introduce a new feature. It turns out that it is relatively easy for an end user to ask for a feature, and often times, end users are surprised when they see their feature show up in the next product release. Generally mature products have lots of features. Vendors exploit this by preparing charts that emphasize their features, while minimizing the features of their competitors. This generally leaves their competitor looking weaker than it might otherwise, but that is just life in the big city. From the end user's perspective though, having lots features does not always equate to happiness. For example, think of how many of the features you typically use in your favorite word processor.

Focus on a dimension for which you are winner. For example, there is often a different winner in each of the following categories: sales volume, years in business, customer service, price, technology, partnerships, financial backers, significant customer wins, and market cap.

Focus on a vertical industry. Vertical marketing targets specific industries, such as the the financial services industry or the travel industry, while horizontal marketing identifies a target audience by common characteristics, such as geography, job title, or the size of the company. By focusing on a vertical industry, a vendor can fill out a product in a such a way as to provide more of a complete solution than is possible when supplying a product to a horizontal segment. There are many vertical industries: for example the North American Industry Classification System uses 6 digits to identify a particular industry. This is good, since it means that there will be many number ones. This is why marketing is so important for companies — without marketing, there would be room for only one number one.

With all these ways of winning, confusion is inevitable. The traditional response has been to produce a two dimensional chart in which the vendor that produces the chart is in the upper right corner and its competitors are to the left and below. For some reason, many people find a certain psychological satisfaction in choosing a vendor in the upper right corner. It is a little bit like eating comfort food after a long, hard day — it may not be good for you, but it does make you feel better for a short while.

Of course, there is a problem from the end user's viewpoint. Users don't care about sub-markets, features, dimensions, or vertical industries. They care about getting their problem solved. They usually have simple expectations: they don't want to spend any money; they don't want the project to take any time; they don't want to have to devote any internal resources; they do want to obtain internal approval; and they would like a solution created specifically for them. Sometimes their expectations are not met.

Naively, you might expect that this tension between the desires of vendors and the needs of customers creates a problem. But that is not the way it works. Rather, it creates an opportunity. Consultants exist to exploit this opportunity; industry analysts and pundits exist to write about it; and, each year, new companies are started and promise that they will change things.

3.6 Why Clutter Is Inevitable

Products are built by companies and companies usually survive by competing in one of only a few basic ways:

- *By Price.* A company can sell a less expensive product than its competitors. Think of Wal-Mart and its promise of "always low prices."

- *By Service.* A company can provide better service than its competitors. Think of Hertz. It can charge more for its cars because it provides a higher level of customer service. Its cars all have four wheels and are essentially the same as those of its competitors.

- *By Technical Leadership.* A company can sell a product by providing better performance or functionality than its competitors. Bose's tag line is "better sound through research." For example, in 1989 it introduced noise canceling acoustic headsets for airplane pilots. Fifteen years later, it's common to see them being used by frequent travelers.

- *By Brand.* A company can sell its product by building its brand. For example, polo tee shirts from Brooks Brothers are not very different from those of many of its competitors, but are more expensive because of the Brooks Brothers brand. Given the clutter in the market place, many purchases are simply made based upon the brand.

Most companies will attempt to position themselves as a leader in at least of one of these categories. Because of this, instead of having one *leader* for each industry; instead, each industry tends to have multiple leaders, a *price leader*, *technical leader*, etc.

As mentioned in the last section, one strategy companies use to position themselves as a leader is to begin with a market and to make it more and more narrow until their company emerges as the clear leader. A simple "back of the envelope" computation gives some idea of what to expect. Consider a Market X with the following properties:

- The size of Market X is about \$1B per year.

- Seventy-five percent of the market is controlled by the three largest vendors.

- The revenue of the smaller vendors (i.e. not one of the top three) in Market X varies between $20–$100 Million, with an average revenue of $50 Million year.

If 75% or $750 Million of the market is controlled by the three largest vendors, this leaves about $250 Million to be split among all the other vendors. A good strategy in a case like this, is for one or more of the smaller vendors to position the $250 Million fragment as a new market, in which it can be the leader. These dynamics tend to split markets into smaller and smaller markets, in which it is easier for the companies to compete.

For example, different analysts split the data warehouse (DW) market into a number of sub-markets, including, for example, Query & Reporting (QR), Executive Information Systems (EIS), On Line Analytic Processing (OLAP), and Extraction, Transformation, & Loading (ETL). In addition, there are other markets which overlap the data warehousing market, including Decision Support Systems (DSS), Customer Relationship Management (CRM), Supply Chain Management (SCM), Business Intelligence (BI), Data Mining (DM), Knowledge Management (KM), and Enterprise Resource Planning (ERP). Each vendor in each sub-market must claim leadership each year to stay competitive. Therefore, in this example, instead of three leaders in the data warehousing market, you have three leaders in each of the 4 sub-markets, along 5 dimensions (namely, market share, price, service, technical leadership and brand). This gives

- 3 leaders x 4 sub-markets x 5 dimensions = 60 leaders, instead of three leaders in data warehousing per se; and, another

- 3 leaders x 7 related sub-markets x 5 dimensions = 105 leaders in the 7 overlapping markets.

Even if the marketing team and its consultants for each of these companies takes weekends off and an occasional vacation, there is plenty of opportunity to create clutter.

As just one contributing factor, instead of one acronym (DW), there are now 12 acronyms (DW, QR, EIS, OLAP, etc.) No wonder there is market clutter.

3.7   Who Clutters

> An expert is someone who knows some of the worst mistakes that can be made in his subject, and how to avoid them.

> Werner Heisenberg (1901-1976), Physics and Beyond, 1971.

> To be an analyst you basically have to be an egomaniac, number one, and obnoxious, number two.

> Charlie Gulotta, head of analyst relations for IBM Global Services, quoted in Christopher Kock, Under Influence, Darwin Magazine, March, 2001.

Understanding the nature of marketing clutter is easier with a better understanding of who clutters. Clutter comes from a number of sources.

Vendors.   Vendors provide products and services to the market place. There are over 600 publicly traded software companies. If each one puts out just 15 press releases a year, that results in about 9000 press releases a year. Vendors produce clutter for the simple reason that their job is to create market niches in which they are in the top right hand corner. Since all the other vendors are doing the same thing, marketing clutter results.

Technology Analysts.   There are several different types of industry and financial analysts, including analysts from market research firms, brokerage firms, investment banks, and firms that supply data. Industry analysts also benefit from market clutter since their job, in part, is to sort through the clutter and to speculate about which companies they expect to do well, which companies they expected to make their numbers, and which companies they expect to miss their numbers. The higher the visibility of analysts, the happier their employers are. This has a tendency to encourage some analysts to be a bit more controversial than they might otherwise be.

Pundits. In addition, there are individuals who track the space and report on it. They write columns, opinion pieces, and reviews. They also benefit from clutter since their job is to sort through it in an entertaining fashion. It is useful to keep in mind that many pundits are naturally interested in attracting as large an audience as possible, and, for that reason, are often as interested in entertaining as in informing.

Consultants. Consultants benefit from clutter since they are paid by the hour to sort it out. In other words, they have little incentive to reduce clutter.

The technology research industry started soon after computers started being sold. At the beginning, these companies sold data about the market size and vendor share to technology companies and to Wall Street. In 1979, Gideon Gartner started a company with a different focus — selling research and analyst face time to companies who needed help selecting technology and to vendors who wanted insights into their markets. By 2001, Gartner had expanded to over 4000 employees in 90 locations, did $952 million in revenues, and was part of a market segment with over $2B of yearly revenue.

The role of a technology analyst has the potential for conflict. The reason is simple. Technology analysts have a natural tendency to recommend vendors that they know well. The easiest way for a company to get contact with an analyst is for the company to purchase products and services from the research company that employs the analyst.

Today, end users often base decisions upon the advice of consultants, industry analysts, and pundits. In some ways, this is not all that different than the way that Roman soldiers in the seventh century B.C.E. prophesied the future using entrails of animals (see, for example [150]). It may be not always work, but it is not so bad until a better technology comes along.

3.8   Sources of Clutter: Features

In this section, we walk through an example of how a business might make a technology decision in order to gain a better understanding of why there is so much clutter in the market. Here is the basic idea: technology is often selected using lists of features. Hence, from this perspective, the more features a product contains the more likely someone is to buy it. Clutter quickly follows.

Here is a simple example. An important activity these days is making lists. A related activity is checking off items in a list. Both require technology, and unfortunately, the choice of technology is not obvious, and, depending upon the technical requirements, a ball point, fountain pen, or pencil may be required.

Here is a common process that a business might use to select new technology. First, technical requirements are gathered (each requirement becomes a column in a table). Next the technical requirements are used to develop a request for proposals (RFP) which are sent to potential vendors. The proposals that are returned are then evaluated and one is selected. Finally, a contract process is started in order to purchase the technology selected. This can take months.

There is a great deal of risk, though, with this approach. Even in this simple example, there are three choices. On average with a random guess, the wrong technology would be selected 2/3 of the time or about 66% of the time. In my experience, many companies select the wrong technology much more frequently than they would if they just guessed.

For this reason, an external consultant is generally used

to issue a report containing a product feature table (product feature tables are described below). The consultant can then take the blame if the project fails. It is usually important to use a large firm, since one is paying for safety and not the quality of advice. There is more safety with a large, well-recognized firm, since its sheer size means that others are obtaining the same advice from the consultants, and the methods being used are more likely to be standard industry practice, even if they are wrong. Therefore, you cannot be fired for relying on their advice. Of course, large firms have higher overheads and cost much more than smaller firms.

A product feature table is a table with each row containing a different product and each column containing a different feature. There are three sample product feature tables below: one from a pencil vendor's perspective, one from a ball point pen vendor's perspective, and one from a fountain pen vendor's perspective. Notice that each table selects a different combination of features so that their preferred product ends up in the upper right corner of the table. This is usually not hard: selecting the features "ease of use" and "erasable" works for pencils; selecting the features "ease of maintenance" and "permanent" works for ball point pens; while, selecting the features "impact" and "permanent" works for fountain pens.

One of the reasons for clutter is now clear. Essentially the same information is in each of these tables — it is simply presented in slightly different way in the pencil table (pencils are erasable) compared to the pen table (pens are permanent). As the technology becomes less familiar, it becomes harder and harder to see through this type of repackaging.

Of course, technologies selected in this way usually require training, and generally training is supplied by the vendor, usually for an additional price. This is true with this example also. If you buy an expensive pen, the clerk is always happy to teach you how to use it.

	Create Lists	Ease of Use	Erasable
Pencil	Yes	Easy: Ready to Use	Yes
Ball Point Pen	Yes	Medium: Click or Twist Required	No
Fountain Pen	Yes	Difficult: Easily Broken	No

Table 3.2:   A feature list for a vendor selling pencils. Clearly, a sensible person would buy a pencil.

	Create Lists	Maintenance	Permanent
Ball Point Pen	Yes	Easy to Maintain: Refill Cartridges	Yes
Fountain Pen	Yes	Difficult to Maintain: Must Refill	Yes
Pencil	Yes	Cannot Maintain: Must Replace	No

Table 3.3: A feature list for a vendor selling ball point pens. Clearly, a sensible person would buy a ball point pen.

	Create Lists	Impact	Permanent
Fountain Pen	Yes	High: Conveys Quality	Yes
Ball Point Pen	Yes	Medium: Neutral Impression	Yes
Pencil	Yes	Low: Negative Impression	No

Table 3.4: A feature list for a vendor selling fountain pens. Clearly, a sensible person would buy a fountain pen.

Clutter comes not only from these three separate tables, but also from all the other tables produced by consultants, columnists, reviewers, and industry analysts produced from these. For example, given these three tables, the Table 3.5 is a a typical summary. Note that the scores are computed to two decimal points conveying great confidence in their validity. On the other hand, the inputs are rather quirky, to say the least. For example, a pencil is assigned a score of 1 (the worst) for maintenance since the reviewer has decided that it is very bad that pencils cannot be maintained but instead must be replaced. On the other hand, another reviewer might decide that this is very good — after all the cost is very low — and assign the pencil a score of 3 for maintenance. This would increase the score of the pencil to 2.33, tying it for first. In this circumstance, a second consultant is usually brought in to sort everything out.

Although this example may seem far-fetched, this is only because the technology is so familiar. The same process is used to evaluate hardware, software, networking and data technologies in general. Clutter comes from the process, from the number of features considered, and from the presentation. As the number of features increases, the process becomes more and more arbitrary. This is to the advantage of many of the participants and feature lists generally become quite long. For example, Crystal Reports, which is used for generating reports from a data warehouse, provided a feature list for their product that was five pages long and contained over 150 features.

3.9 A Case Study in Innovation: Databases

We turn now from looking at market clutter to looking at technical innovation. The next three sections each contain a case study about innovation. This section contains a case study in innovation that describes some of the innovations that have taken place in data management over the past 50

	Create Lists	Ease of Use	Maint.	Erasable
Ball Point Pen	3	2	3	1
Fountain Pen	3	1	2	1
Pencil	3	3	1	3

	Impact	Perm.	Score
Ball Point Pen	2	3	2.33
Fountain Pen	3	3	2.16
Pencil	1	1	2.00

Table 3.5: A feature list as prepared by a consultant. Note that the scores are computed to two decimal points conveying great confidence in their validity. On the other hand, the evaluations are often rather odd, like the assignment of the lowest score of 1 to a pencil for maintenance since a traditional pencil cannot be refilled. Another reviewer might decide on the other hand that this is a positive, making the pencil very easy to maintain, and assign a score of 3. This would increase the pencil's over all score to a 2.33, tying it for first.

years. This topic is mature enough that there is a broad consensus on what some of the major innovations are. We describe the consensus history, which, by and large, follows a paper of Jim Gray [55].

One hundred years of data processing. During the last one hundred years or so, data processing has gone through five major periods.

1. In the first period (1900-1960), data was stored on punched cards. The data was processed by mechanical or electrical machines that read the punched cards and tabulated various quantities. As an example, the 1890 US Census used punched cards and electrical tabulators.

2. In the second period (1955-1970), data was stored on magnetic tapes. The data was processed by programs that read the tapes and computed various quantities, possibly writing new tapes. A typical application of this technology was direct mailing.

3. In the third period (1965-1985), the first databases were introduced, which abstracted and standardized some of the operations performed on data. In this period, data was stored on-line using disks. A typical application was an airline reservation system.

4. In the fourth period (1980-2000), relational databases were introduced and client server systems became common. Today, relational databases are ubiquitous, with millions of such systems now deployed. Together, Oracle, IBM, and Microsoft sell over $12 Billion of relational databases per year.

5. Currently, we are in the fifth period (1995-present). Today's databases can store not just tables of numbers but also a variety of media types, including documents, images, audio, and video. A typical application is to support an online order system containing pricing data, catalog images, and inventory levels.

Punched Cards: 1900–1960. As discussed in more detail in Section 1.11, the 1890 US Census used punched cards to manage the data that was collected. Each household was encoded in a different card, and electro-mechanical machines would read the cards and tabulate the number of people in blocks, census tracts, congressional districts, and states. Programming was done by re-wiring patch panels (similar to an old fashioned telephone switch board). The results of one computation could be written onto new punch cards, to be used as input for another computation.

Although quaint by today's standards, using punched cards and tabulating machines was an order of magnitude faster and could handle several orders of magnitude more data than the hand systems used previously.

A company started by Herman Hollerith, which provided the punched card technology, eventually became IBM. IBM supplied punched card technology to business and government customers from 1915–1960. Punched cards survived for a quite a few years after that. I was using them for the programs that I wrote in 1972.

Batch Processing of Tapes: 1955–1970. The second period saw several major innovations. Data was stored on tapes, instead of punch cards. 1n 1951, the Census Department accepted delivery of the first UNIVAC computer developed by the Remington Rand Corporation. This was the first general purpose computer to use magnetic tape. A single magnetic tape could hold as much information as ten thousand punched cards. Tapes could be read and written at 12,800 characters per second.

In this period, software was developed to process records stored on tape. The preliminary design of the computer language COBOL was completed in the period June to December, 1959. COBOL was the first general purpose computer language for processing business data. A typical COBOL application would read several input files from disk or tape and write an output file to disk or tape [130].

In this period, file systems were introduced and used to

store the records, and a job control language was introduced to run the jobs.

The first batch processing systems were also introduced in this period. Transactions about records were recorded throughout the day. Typically, once a day all the records were sorted by key and all the records associated with a given key were collected and used to update the master file with that key. Batch systems are efficient and still used to this day. For example, many systems for producing lists in direct marketing still use files of transactions which are processed in batch to produce updated master files.

Batch systems had several draw backs. First, errors in transaction data were not usually detected until the batch run and could take some time to correct. Second, the database was never current except for the brief period after the batch run.

Online Network Databases: 1965–1985. Batch processing of transactions to update master files was well suited to a variety of applications ranging from direct marketing to preparing credit card statements. Since credit card statements are sent out once a month, and direct mail campaigns are typically sent out several times a year, using a batch system was adequate.

On the other hand, some important applications such as airline reservation systems, stock market trading systems, and defense systems require immediate access to the most current data. To handle these types of applications, systems that became known as online transaction processing or OLTP systems began to be developed. These consisted of a variety of components, including distributed terminals for accessing the systems and Teleprocessing Monitors (TPs) that collected the requests from the possibly hundreds of distributed terminals and queued them to the component that accessed the data on line.

Data was arranged in records and stored in secondary storage, such as magnetic disks, and could be accessed in less than a second. The OLTP allowed a terminal to access a few records, update them, and return the result. Data records were accessed by *key*, a unique number assigned to each record. Specialized data structures and programs were developed to access large collections of records by key.

At this time, it was becoming common to view data not only as consisting of records, but also as the *associations* or links between records. For example, in an airline reservation system, a city was linked with all the flights that left the city. A flight was linked with the passengers having a reservation on the flight. A customer was linked with the flights for which he held a reservation. Rather than storing data records in flat files, data could now be accessed first by key, and then by associations by following the appropriate links. This was a major innovation.

During this period, the COBOL community created a Data Base Task Group (DBTG) to define standards for accessing data. One of the outcomes was the concept of *schemas*. A database had a logical schema that defined the fields in records and the associations between records. A database also had a physical schema that defined the physical layout of data on disks and indices that are needed to access the data efficiently. Finally a program could have a sub-schema defining just the fields required by the program. Although a simple idea, the separation of logical and physical structures was one of the innovations that created the modern database.

The ability for many distributed terminals to access and update the database also created new problems. The database could become inconsistent if two terminals tried to update the database at the same time. Another key innovation introduced at this time was the concept of a transaction. A database *transaction* allowed an update to lock a record for a period of time so that other processes could access it but not update it. Transactions were also logged and procedures put in place so that if the database were to fail a consistent version of the database could be reconstructed from the transaction log.

Relational Databases: 1980–2000. Developing programs for network databases required programmers to write code that explicitly navigated the links between records. This presented an important trade-off — the code executed very efficiently but was difficult to write.

An alternative was provided by the relational data model, which was introduced in a fundamental 1970 paper by E. F. Codd, who was working at IBM [33].

With a relational data model, data can be thought of as distributed between one or more tables, with links formed between records using identifiers called *keys*. For example, an Employee ID or EID can be used to link one table containing employee names and addresses, a second table containing employee salaries, and a third table containing an employee's department and the name of his or hers supervisor. With this approach, when an employee moves and the database is updated with his or her new address, only one record needs to be updated. The other tables access the new address implicitly using the EID key, instead of explicitly using links of network databases. This was a nice advantage provided by relational databases compared to network databases.

Another advantage of a relational database was that programmers could use higher level abstractions to access data, allowing them to write programs and queries more quickly and efficiently. The trade-off, though, was that the programs were sometimes less efficient than programs using network databases. Indeed, initially there was a fair amount of skepticism whether relational databases would ever be fast enough to replace network databases.

In contrast, accessing data with network databases is done using procedural languages, such as COBOL. With procedural languages, the programmer explicitly describes how to follow links from one data record to another. Accessing data with relational databases is done using declarative languages, such as the Structured Query Language or SQL, which was developed and standardized by a group at IBM in the 1970's. With SQL, one simply specifies the tables containing the data, the columns one wants, and any operations, such as joining two or more tables, how the rows should be ordered, and how the rows should be grouped. The database itself then turns this declarative description of the query to code that can be executed to retrieve the data.

Over time, relational databases became more efficient and people querying databases became much smarter about how to organize data in relational databases efficiently and how to write queries in SQL efficiently. Today, relational databases are ubiquitous.

Recent Developments: 1995-today.   Recently, databases have been extended in several important ways. First, more complex data can be stored in databases today, including text, XML documents, images, videos, multimedia documents, and data types defined by users. Although these types of data are now common, there is always a lag as a mature technology, like databases, adopt to support them.

Second, databases are being extended to work with data that is distributed over more than one computer and over more than location. During the period of network databases and relational databases, network bandwidth was limited and, by and large, only user queries and the response to queries were transported over networks. Today, more and more systems are being deployed over networks with much more abundant bandwidth, and it is now possible for distributed databases to also move the underlying data over the network.

Third, databases now allow users not only to define their own data types but also their own functions. In this context, functions are computer programs that take input data, process it, and produce output data. Today, data and functions are often combined together to create what are called objects, and databases have been extended to support these.

Since we are still in the middle of this period, rather

than speculate any more about it, it would perhaps be best to wait another ten years or so, and then look back.

3.10   A Case Study in Innovation: Searching for Primes

This case study is about determining whether a number is prime. One of the interesting things about this case study is the very long period of time over which continuous progress has been made, beginning with the work by the Greeks in the third Century BC. We begin by reviewing what a prime number is.

The set of counting numbers 1, 2, 3, ... divides naturally into two classes of numbers: numbers, such as 12, that can be factored into a products of smaller numbers, for example:

$$12 = 2 \times 2 \times 3.$$

and numbers such as 37 that have no such factorization. A number from the latter class of numbers is called a *prime* number, and a number from the former class is called a *composite* number.

Prime numbers have fascinated people for a long time. Important results about prime numbers were proved by Greek mathematicians who were part of the Pythagorean School during the period 500–300 BC. About 300 BC, Euclid published several important results about primes, including a proof that there are an infinite number of primes (i.e. there is no largest prime) and that every integer can be written essentially uniquely as a product of primes.

Sieve of Eratosthenes. One of the first innovations in the search for large primes is due to Eratosthenes, who lived from 276 BC–194 BC. It is called the Sieve Method and it is simple to describe. First, make a list of counting numbers as in the first row of Table 3.6. Begin, by removing 1 from the list since it is not prime. Continue, by removing every second number after 2, since each of these numbers is divisible by 2. This produces row 2 of Table 3.6. Next, remove every third number after 3, since each of these numbers is divisible by 3. This produces row 3 of Table 3.6.

Continuing in this way, we are left with only the primes remaining. In the example above, the numbers remaining are 2, 3, 5, 7, 11, and 13 and these are all the primes less than 15. Given enough paper (or papyrus) and enough time, it is straightforward to write long lists of primes.

1	2	3	4	5	6	7	8	9	10	11	12	13	14	15
-	2	3	-	5	-	7	-	9	-	11	-	13	-	15
-	2	3	-	5	-	7	-	-	-	11	-	13	-	-

Table 3.6: The Sieve of Eratosthenes is used to compute prime numbers. The first row shows the sieve at the start, and the second row shows the sieve after 1 and all multiples of 2 are removed. The third row shows the sieve after all multiples of 3 are removed.

It is easy to write a computer program that implements this algorithm. For example, in the notes there is an eleven line Python program that computes primes in this way. Using this program, I can compute on my laptop all the primes less than or equal to 250,000 in a second or so. By the way, there are 22,044 of them — try it.

If all the primes smaller than a fixed number are needed — say all the primes less than 1,000,000 — then the Sieve Method (and its variants) is still the best way to find them. This is not bad for an algorithm that is over 2000 years old.

Mersenne Primes. Numbers of the form

$$M_n = 2 \times 2 \times 2 \cdots \times 2 - 1, \qquad (2 \text{ occurs } n \text{ times})$$

are called *Mersenne Numbers*. If a Mersenne number M_n is prime, it is called a *Mersenne Prime*. For a small prime numbers n, Mersenne Numbers are prime, which led to the mistaken belief that they are prime for all n. They are named after Marin Mersenne, who was a French monk living from 1588–1648. In the preface to his book Cogitata Physica-Mathematica (1644), Mersenne claimed that Mersenne numbers were primes for $n = 2, 3, 5, 7, 13, 17, 19, 31, 67, 127$ and 257 and were composite for all other positive integers $n < 257$. This is not true as the table below shows, but as usual, the names that are used in technology are not usually closely connected to those who deserve the most credit.

Today, many people devote unused computing cycles of their PCs to a project called GIMPS that uses loosely connected clusters of PCs to compute Mersenne Primes.

Although outside the scope of the book, a lot of innovative mathematics and computer science has been created to study primes and to discover the largest primes.

3.11 A Case Study in Innovation: Routing Packets

This case study is about the networking infrastructure that made the Internet possible. The story begins in the early 1960's. To provide context, it is helpful to compare the Internet to the telephone network, which is how we begin.

The Internet is in a certain sense like an inside-out telephone network. The telephone network (until recently) consisted of inexpensive, easy to use devices (telephones) connected to an expensive, intelligent, homogeneous network with good security and central management designed to carry voice. The Internet consists of expensive, hard to use devices (computers) connected to an inexpensive, dumb, heterogeneous network with poor security and distributed management designed to carry data. See Table 3.8.

Here is a simplified description of how data is sent over the (traditional) telephone network. Things are more complicated today, since the same local area code may be split between several area codes, and since cell phones interoperate with the traditional telephone network.

Think of the telephone as a simple device that takes

n	M_n	Digits	Prime?
2	3	1	Prime.
3	7	1	Prime.
5	31	2	Prime.
7	127	3	Prime.
11	2,047	4	Not prime. In 1536 Hudalricus Regius showed that $2047 = 23 * 89$.
13	8,191	4	Prime. Proved prime in 1456. Discover not known.
17	131,071	6	Prime. Cataldi proved prime in 1603 using trial division.
19	524,287	6	Prime. Cataldi proved prime in 1603 using trial division.
23	8,388,607	7	Not prime. Cataldi claimed as prime in 1603. Fermat showed was composite in 1640.
29	536,870,911	8	Not prime. Cataldi claimed as prime in 1603. Euler showed was composite in 1738.
31	2,147,483, 647	10	Prime. Euler proved prime in 1772.
37	137,438,953, 471	12	Not prime. Fermat showed was composite in 1640.
61	2,305,843, 009,213,693, 951	19	Prime. Pervushin proved prime in 1883.

Table 3.7: Mersenne Primes M_n are prime numbers of the form $2 \times 2 \times 2 \cdots \times 2 - 1$, where there are n copies of the number 2. Some M_n are prime and some are not. Source: Chris Caldwell, The Largest Known Prime by Year [27].

your voice and encodes it for transmission over a network. The traditional telephone network consisted of number of circuits. Telephone circuits are set up at the beginning of the call and torn down at the end of the call so that other calls can use them. The telephone network is designed to route a call from the sender, to the sender's local telephone exchange, to the receiver's local telephone exchange, and to the receiver's telephone. The local telephone exchange of the sender and the receiver may be the same, may be connected via a metropolitan network, or may be connected via a long distance network.

Using the telephone number itself, you can determine how the call is routed. The first two or three numbers of a seven digit phone number identify the local telephone exchange. For many years, the telephone exchanges had names such as Wyoming, where the first two letters identified the telephone exchange. Numbers at this exchange would begin 99X-XXXX (W $\leftrightarrow$ 9, Y $\leftrightarrow$ 9). Two telephone exchanges within a metropolitan area specified by an area code are routed using a metropolitan area network, while two telephone exchanges in different areas are routed using the long distance telephone network.

The traditional telephone network required that there be a pair of copper wires from the sender's phone to the local telephone exchange, as well as as from the receiver's phone to his or her local telephone exchange. Between the local exchanges are wires that are shared by many phone calls. To share calls, at switching centers that connect the various local exchanges, the voice signal is time-sliced about 8000 times a second so that the long distance circuits can carry many different phone calls over the same physical wires at the same time.

In the 1960's, during the cold war with the Soviet Union, the United States Department of Defense (DOD) became concerned by the impact of the loss of one or more switching centers, since not only were civilian communications carried by the telephone network but also military communications.

In 1968, the Defense Advanced Projects Agency or DAR-PA, part of DOD, awarded a contract to Bolt Beranket and Newman, Inc. (BBN) to build a new innovative type of communication network, based upon ideas published in the early 1960's for something called packet switching. With packet switching instead of using circuits, data is divided into units called packets. Each packet is labeled with its source address and destination address and sent on the network. Devices on local area networks route the packets from computer to computer and to special devices that became known as *routers* that connect two different local area networks.

With this approach, two different packets might take entirely different routes from the sender to the receiver. A computer on the receiver's end reassembled the different packets. This design was in improvement because the resulting network of networks or Internet was resilient if one or more routers were destroyed.

Over time, several other advantages for this approach began to emerge. For example, since the network was no longer centrally managed, it was relatively inexpensive to connect additional local area networks. One simply added a router between two local area networks. Another advantage was that it was also relatively easy to add new types of applications. Where as the telephone network was designed to carry voice using relatively dumb devices (telephones), the Internet was simply designed to carry data divided into packets using relatively smart edge devices (computers). By writing a new computer application and installing it on two or more computers, new applications could be added to the Internet relatively easily.

	Telephone	Internet
What is the network designed to carry?	voice	data
How is it carried?	using circuits	using packets
Where is the intelligence?	in the network	in the edge devices
Ease of use	easy to use	hard to use
Type of (initial) device	inexpensive consumer device	expensive business device
How are devices specified?	using telephone numbers	using IP numbers
How are local collections of devices specified?	by local telephone exchanges	by network IDs
How are connections made between devices?	using telephone switching centers	using routers
Resiliency	relatively few alternate routings possible	many alternate routings possible
Structure	uniform network	heterogeneous network
Security	secure, security built in	not very secure, security added on

Table 3.8: In some ways, as this table shows, the Internet can be viewed as an inside out telephone network.

Just as a telephone number, say 312-214-1234 consists of an area code (312), an telephone exchange (214), and a device ID specifying a particular phone on the exchange (1234), an IP address specifying a computer consists of different components.

Although IP addresses today work a bit differently, initially they consisted of a 32 bit binary integer that is usually written as four numbers separated by dots, for example, 209.87.112.90. This represents the 32 bit binary integer 11010001 01010111 01110000 01011010.

The IP address is split into two parts. The first part specifies the Network ID, which identifies a specific local area network. The second part, identifies the Host ID, which specifies a particular computer on the local area network. From this point of view, the Internet is simply a large collection of different networks, each specified by a different Network ID. Each network has its own collection of hosts, each of which is specified by a Host ID.

Two networks are connected together by using a special device called a router or gateway, which has an IP address on both networks, and is responsible for moving packets between the different networks as required.

Initially, there were three types of addresses, called Type A (identified by a leading binary 0), Type B (identified by a leading binary 10), and Type C (identified by a leading 110). Type A addresses allocate 7 bits for the Network ID and 24 bits for the Host ID. There is room for 128 type C networks, and each Type C network can have no more than about 16 million hosts. Type B addresses are used for intermediate size networks and devote 14 bits to the Network ID and 16 bits to the Host ID. There is room for about 16,000 type B networks, and each one can have no more than 65,536 hosts. Type C addresses are used for small networks, and allocate 22 bits to the Network ID and 8 bits to the Host ID. There is room for about 4 million type C networks, each with no more than 256 hosts.

For example, the first three bits (110) identify the binary address above as a Class C type address, which means the next 21 bits (10001 01010111 01110000 or 1,136,496) identify the Network ID, and the remaining 8 bits (01011010 or 90) identify the Host ID on the particular network.

Thirty two bit binary addresses provide about 4 billion unique addresses, which was plenty when the Internet was young. But today a large company or university can easily have 10,000 hosts and there is only room for 16,000 such networks around the world. With IPv4, many organizations found themselves without enough public IP addresses. To rectify this shortage of IPv4 addresses, a variety of techniques are used: the addressing scheme today has moved away from simple Type A, B and C addresses to more complicated structure; addresses themselves are moving from 32 bit addresses to larger 128 bit addresses; and many computers are not on the public Internet themselves, but instead on private networks, that are connected to the public Internet using a single IP address.

Sending packets over the network follows a simple procedure. The computer sending the packet examines the packet and compares the source IP address to the destination IP address. There are two possibilities:

1. *The two computers are on the same network.* The sending computer looks at the address of the packet that is being sent and extracts the Internet address of the destination. If the source and target hosts share the same Network ID, then they are are both on the same physical network and the packet can be sent on the local network. The target machine examines all packets sent over the local network and grabs packets with its Host ID.

2. *The two computers are on different networks.* In this case, the source host extracts the Network ID of the destination and uses what is called a routing table. The routing table specifies that packets with certain Network IDs should be forwarded to certain specified gateways for processing. A default gateway is also

specified, which is used for routing any packet that is not a local packet and whose routing is not specified elsewhere in the routing table.

Routing works well for several reasons: First, the routing table can be small and only has to change when new networks are added to the local network. Second, routing decisions can be made by examining just the Network ID of the destination IP. Finally, since routing tables only contain local information, it is relatively easy to keep them up to date.

Chapter 4

Technology Adoption Cycles

4.1 Forces Effecting Technology Adoption

> Scientists seek to understand what is, while engineers seek to create what never was.

Attributed to Theodore von Karman by Henry Petroski

In the prior chapter, we discussed technical innovations and how it is often hard to recognize them immediately from the clutter in the market. In this chapter, we discuss a complementary question. Given a new technology, what are the basic forces that determine how long it takes for the technology to become accepted by the market? Specifically, we discuss four such forces:

- Technology road maps, which chart the trajectory of a technology as it proceeds from basic research to engineering and manufacturing.

- The context that reflects how the new technology integrates with the existing technological base.

- General market forces affecting the vendors developing and marketing the technology.

- The pain and pleasure of users, which determine in part which technologies they purchase and when.

If you have trouble remembering these four forces, think of the initials RCMP for Roadmap, Context, Market forces, and Pain and pleasure. We begin with a brief overview of these four forces.

Technology Roadmaps. The introduction of innovative technology into the market place generally follows a standard trajectory, beginning with basic research, followed in turn by applied research, engineering development, and ending with manufacturing and marketing. A decade or more can elapse from the beginning to the end of this process. For example, Hotmail, the free email service now owned by Microsoft, was launched on July 4, 1996 and two and half years later in February, 1999, it had over 30 million users [89]. From one viewpoint, a subscription base this large after two and a half years is unprecedented, yet from another viewpoint 1999 is 28 years after 1971, the date the first email was sent by Ray Tomlinson, a computer engineer working for Bolt Beranek and Newman in Cambridge, Massachusetts, and eight years after 1991, the date the first web server was developed by Tim Berners-Lee, a software engineer working at CERN in Geneva. This is sometimes summarized as saying that although it is difficult to predict what technology will look like in twenty years, it is certain that if a technology is not in a lab today, then there is not even a possibility that it will be deployed in twenty years.

The Context. A new technology is generally not used alone but almost always integrated with other technologies and business processes. Think of this as the context. Different technologies can have quite different contexts. One way of determining a technology's context is by understanding how a technology integrates into an organization's IT infrastructure and business practices. For example, many companies use Customer Relationship Management (CRM) software to reduce the wait time on the phone for a company's best customers and to provide them with higher quality service when working with them. To implement this requires several steps: first, data must be collected about customers; second, the data must be analyzed in order to develop a useful segmentation of customers; third, this segmentation must be integrated with the telephone system; fourth, the customer service representatives in the call center must be trained; fifth, the process must be maintained over time, as new products and systems are introduced. The complexity of the integration limits the adoption of the technology. In contrast, if a user has a web browser and Internet access, a new web based email account, such as Google's Gmail, Microsoft's Hotmail or Yahoo! Mail, can be set up in less than five minutes. This simplicity was one of the reasons that Hotmail was able to build up a user base so quickly. From the perspective of context, one of the reasons that web based email took off so quickly is because it took off in a vacuum compared to other applications, such as back office and front office applications.

Market Forces.   It is likely that both web-based email and CRM software will be used in 10 years. On the other hand, it is also likely that many of the vendors providing the software will be different. A variety of market forces determine the fate of technology vendors, many unrelated to the the technology itself. Vendors get acquired, make acquisitions, introduce new product lines, shed old product lines, make $1B revenue errors on their SEC filings, etc. From the viewpoint of a technology user, it is not a bad approximation to assume that the adoption of a new technology is determined by the technology roadmap and by the context. In contrast, the entrance and exit of technology vendors into and out of the market can perhaps best be viewed as a random walk. To say it another way, it is relatively easy to predict that CRM technologies and web based email will enter the market, as well as the velocity of their adoption, but relatively hard to predict which particular vendors will be marketing these technologies. Businesses pay a lot of money to experts to hear about market forces, but this will not change these facts, it simply makes businesses feel a little bit better.

The Pain and Pleasure of Users. Users usually buy new technology for one of two reasons: it solves a problem by addressing a pain they currently have in their work, such as reducing the time to fill out a travel expense form from fifteen minutes to five minutes, or it provides pleasure, such as an audio hard disk jukebox, which can store 1000 songs and fit into a shirt pocket.

The conventional wisdom is that a good company with a good CEO can get a mediocre product into the market. In contrast, the point of view here is that which technologies enter the market is primarily a factor of the technology trajectory and the context. Given the right trajectory and the right context, a technology will most likely reach the market. In most cases, a market, or more accurately, a market segment, is dominated by three to four vendors. One should perhaps be a bit cautious when drawing conclusions based upon the characteristics of the surviving companies and their CEOs lest one falls victim to post hoc ergo propter hoc.

4.2   The Basic Equation of Marketing

The chasm is, by any measure, a very bad place to be.

Geoffrey A. Moore, Crossing the Chasm, HarperBusiness, New York, New York, 1991, page 63.

This section introduces a very simple model of technology adoption that is summarized in Tables 4.1 and 4.2. One of the factors in this model is the approximate size of an existing or potential market. One way of estimating this is to multiply the estimated Average Selling Price (ASP) of the product or service by the estimated number of units sold each year (Unit Sales).

Market ($/year) = Average Selling Price ($/unit) × Units Sold per Year (units/year).

This equation places companies in different cells, as indicated in the Table 4.1. In this table, there are 12 cells spread over three columns (labeled $1M, $10M and $100M) and four rows (labeled $100, $1000, $10,000 and $100,000). Each cell has quite different characteristics and challenges. For example, if a product costs about $1000, then a ten thousand units per year must be sold for the company to have a yearly revenue of about $10 million, the approximate revenue target for a technology company considering entering the public markets before the Internet bubble temporarily lowered the threshold. A company with $1 million has about 10 employees and one level of management. A company with $10 million of revenue has about 100 employees and two to three levels of management. Every time a company doubles or triples in size, it must change the way it does business, and it must change many of its underlying business processes.

If you talk to someone who sells technology products, you quickly realize that some people like to buy products as soon as they enter the market, others like to wait until *someone* else they know has bought the product, others like to wait until *many* people they know have bought the product, while others like to wait until *everyone* else they know has bought the product. One of the things that survived the Internet bubble is catchy names for these categories of users: they are generally called innovators, early adopters, the main street market, and laggards.

From this perspective, many companies tend to fall into one of four groups, as illustrated by the four rows in the Table 4.1. For example, the challenge of a software company selling department level software applications, such as databases, is to get several hundred innovators to adopt their product, followed by several thousand early adopters,

ASP	$1M AR	$10M AR	$100M AR
$100	10,000	100,000	1,000,000
$1,000	1,000	10,000	100,000
$10,000	100	1,000	10,000
$100,000	10	100	1,000
	Innovators	**Early Adopters**	**Main Street**

Table 4.1: It is sometimes helpful to view companies as falling into one of four broad categories, determined by the average selling price (ASP) of their product or service. In the table above, there are separate rows for an ASP of $100, $1,000, $10,000 and $100,000. As companies grow in revenue, they face a number of difficult transitions in their operations and in their marketing. The table above considers three stages: when a company's annual revenue (AR) is $1M, $10M and $100M. The type of customers who buy new technology changes as the technology grows more mature and becomes more familiar. The terms innovators, early adopters, main street, and laggards were introduced in [92] to describe some of these different groups of customers. The middle columns in the table above show the number of units that must be sold each year to reach sales of $1M, $10M and $100M.

and continuing on to the main street market of tens of thousands of customers.

As the table indicates, the target user for each row is different. In technology, individuals usually purchase items that cost a few hundred dollars; small offices or home offices (SOHO) usually purchase items that cost several thousand dollars; small companies or departments within larger companies usually purchase items that cost $10,000, while larger companies (enterprises) usually purchase items that cost $100,000.

Although each of the transitions from one column to the next is difficult and requires a different marketing strategy, the transition from the market of early adopters to the main street market is generally extremely challenging and has become known as the chasm. The name is from an influential marketing book of the 1990's written by Geoffrey A. Moore called *Crossing the Chasm* [92], which focused on this transition.

ASP	Innovators	Early Adopters	Early Majority	Late Majority	Late Adopters	Laggards	
100	30,000	130,000	340,000	340,000	130,000	30,000	individual
1000	3,000	13,000	34,000	34,000	13,000	3,000	SOHO
10,000	300	1,300	3,400	3,400	1,300	300	dept.
100,000	30	130	340	340	130	30	enterprise
AR	3M	13M	34M	34M	13M	3M	100M
AR/TR	3%	13%	34%	34%	13%	3%	100%
Years	3	2	2	2	2	3	14

Table 4.2: A slightly more sophisticated model of the technology adoption cycle for a product with a total revenue (TR) of $100,000,000 over a lifetime of 14 years in which the annual revenues (AR) follow a bell-like curve. The first four rows of data show the relationship between the average selling price (ASP) and the number of units sold (Units Sold) to reach the annual revenues indicated. The seventh row of the table shows the percentage of the revenue that year compared to the total lifetime revenue. Each market (innovators, early adopters, early majority, etc.) has its own psychology so that there are gaps between the market strategies required for the different segments. The gap between the early adopters and the early majority is sometimes particularly wide, and has become known as the chasm.

We close this section by showing how Tables 4.1 and 4.2 can be used to provide a back of the envelope understanding of the economic constraints on new products. Here is a simple example, sometimes called Bill's Law, after Bill Joy, the Co-Founder and Chief Scientist at Sun Microsystems. Bill (Joy)'s Law: "Don't write software for less than 100,000 platforms." One hundred thousand unit sales at $1000/unit generates $100,000,000 of revenue per year. Ten percent of this is $10,000,000/year, which is enough to support about a hundred engineers. In 2001, Sun did over $18B in revenue and had over 43,000 employees.

Here is another simple example, sometimes called Bill's Law, after Bill Gates, the Chairman and co-founder of Microsoft. Compare Bill (Gate)'s Law: "Don't write software for less than 1,000,000 platforms." One million unit sales at $100/unit generates about $100,000,000 of revenue per year. As before, ten percent of this is $10,000,000/year, which is enough to support about a hundred engineers. In 2001, Microsoft did about $25B in revenue, and had over 47,000 employees.

4.3   Getting to Main Street

> Technology has the shelf life of a banana. By the time you buy it, implement it and train people on it, it's obsolete. The right thing to do is to share IP. Rather than litigate and protect our IP, we've decide to innovate and share it.
>
> Scott McNealy (1954 –), Co-founder and Chairman of
> Sun Microsystems.

A popular measure of the adoption of technology in the consumer technology market is the number of years it takes a new technology to reach a million users. In "market speak," once this occurs, the technology is said to have reached Main Street. An interesting comparison is provided by the automotive industry. The first automobiles were introduced in about 1902 and by 1914 there were over a million registered automobiles, which was about 1% of the US population at that time. While AOL cost about $20/month and Hotmail was free, an automobile in 1914 cost about $2000, which is about $36,000 in today's dollars.

One way of looking at Main Street is in terms of market penetration. Think of the approximate size of the US market for consumer goods and services as about 300 million individuals. Then a user base of 3 million is equivalent to a market penetration of about 1%. Since the size of markets can be hard to estimate, knowing the absolute number of new users each year and total user base is an alternative metric that is also frequently used.

Companies take a variety of paths, usually involving many detours, to reach Main Street. Everyone likes winners: winners tend to be written about and remembered, while those coming in second or third tend to be ignored. A famous example of a technology company that reached Main Street fairly quickly is Sun Microsystems. It reached Main Street in just six years after it was founded in 1982. By 1988, Sun reached revenues of $1B/year by selling approximately 100,000 computer workstations at about ten thousand dollars per unit [137]. There are a number of things to be cautious about when viewing technology from this perspective. Perhaps the most important is to be aware that there is usually a significant gap between the introduction of a new technology into the market place and the emergence of a company that carries the technology to Main Street. Usually several vendors enter and leave the market before one any of them reach Main Street. It is common to view this as a failure to market correctly; on the other hand, it is perhaps better viewed as a mistake in entering the market too early. The trajectory of a technology as it follows a technology road map is usually quite long, often time taking a decade or two; predicting the general time period within a few years of when a technology is ready to reach Main Street is fairly easy; predicting the particular year is much harder. Unfortunately, it is the latter which is often a critical success factor for a technology vendor.

From a marketing perspective, reaching Main Street is critical, since as can be seen from Table 4.2, most of a company's revenues (and, it is hoped profits) come during this period. For the hypothetical company in the table that has a product in the market for 14 years, 68% of the revenues come during the 4 years it is on Main Street. On the other hand, most of the development costs occur during the preceding 5 years, and these development years are often unprofitable.

For successful technologies, although several companies will reach Main Street, predicting which companies reach it is generally not easy. An important factor is when they enter the market. The closer the entry point to the inflection point in the roadmap, the more likely the company is to reach Main Street. Companies entering too early often don't have the staying power; companies entering too late often don't have the marketing power to displace the current market leaders.

Analyzing products and vendors from this point of view is complicated by several factors: using the hypothetical example above covering the 14 year history of a product ignores the fact that over this period, a product undergoes a number of significant changes and it is perhaps simply a matter of convenience whether to consider these as evolutions of a single product or as genuinely new products.

Another complicating factor is that most companies that have a product on Main Street also sell and market a number of other products. Each of these other products may be building towards Main Street, on Main Street, or transitioning off Main Street.

We conclude this section with a final observation. Just as there are two views of the stock market — some feel that the prices of individual stocks cannot be predicted, with the fluctuations in prices most accurately modeled as a random walk, while others feel that the behavior of individual stocks can be predicted by experts — there are two views of vendors.

One view of vendors, championed by the analysts who track them, is that with a proper knowledge of the space, one can predict which vendors will prosper, which will fail, and which will limp along. Another view, less common, is to model the progress of vendors as a random walk.

Viewing vendors in this way highlights an important factor complicating the adoption of new technology — the lack of stability of the vendors that supply new technology due to market forces (the "M" in the acronym RCMP introduced at the beginning of this chapter).

Despite these complications, the basic facts are clear, and it is useful to summarize them here again: Predicting technology breakthroughs is difficult; identifying technology breakthroughs is much easier. Predicting which particular vendors will reach Main Street is difficult; predicting technology trajectories based upon technology road maps is much easier. From this perspective, understanding the adoption of a new technology is relatively easy to understand, whether it is an automobile at the beginning of the last century or the Internet at the end of the last century.

4.4 Case Study: The Nike Pegasus

The adoption of any new technology, including the technology in running shoes, depends upon a complex interaction between the usefulness of the technology, the savvy of the marketing, and the receptivity of the user base. New technology creates opportunities, but without the push provided by innovative marketing and the pull of a cohesive user base, technology is not adopted but rather simply evaporates over time.

Nike's shoes are branded with a swoosh and were endorsed by Michael Jordan. The company was started in 1964 and by 1987 had developed four generations of the Air Pegasus and sold five million of them. Nike is generally considered to be a marketing success. On closer examination, it is just as noteworthy as a technology success. In

Year	Production	Registration
1900	4,192	8,000
1902	9,000	23,000
1904	22,130	54,590
1906	33,200	105,900
1908	63,500	194,400
1910	181,000	458,377
1912	356,000	901,596
1914	548,139	1,664,003
1916	1,525,578	3,367,889

Table 4.3: The mass production of automobiles started in 1908 with the Model T Ford. Within six years, over one million automobiles had been registered. Within eight years, over one million automobiles were being produced a year. Source: Facts and Figures, Automobile Manufacturers Association, New York, New York, 1950. Also, Encyclopedia Britannica, Motor Cars, Volume 15, page 881, Encyclopedia Britannica, Inc., Chicago, 1957.

fact, it is a company that provides an example of a rare combination of marketing and technology innovation.

Bill Bowerman was one of the co-founders of the company, which was originally called Blue Ribbon Sports or BRS. He was the University of Oregon track coach from 1944-1972, and while he was there, his teams won four NCAA team championships and he coached 44 All Americans and 19 Olympians. He observed that every ounce shaved from a shoe decreased by 200 pounds the weight lifted by his runners in a typical race [105]. In 1967, Bowerman began development of BRS's Marathon, which was one of the first running shoes made from lightweight nylon.

The year 1971 was a pivotal one for the company, both from a marketing and a technological viewpoint. In 1971, according to company lore, Jeff Johnson, the company's first employee, had a dream the night before the first shoe boxes were to be printed. The dream was about Nike, the Greek goddess of victory, and created the identity for the company. Phil Knight, the other co-founder of the company, wanted to call the company Dimension 6, a name that was no doubt too technical to make it a main stream marketing success.

In the same year 1971, Bowerman, while eating waffles at breakfast, got the inspiration for what later became Nike's waffle sole. He prototyped the sole by pouring urethane rubber into his family's waffle iron and then worked hard for the next several years perfecting it. By 1974, the Nike's Waffle trainer had become the best selling training shoes in the United Sates, and his wife had forgiven him for ruining the waffle iron.

When reading accounts about marketing, it is common to hear about inspirations from dreams, eureka moments while taking showers, and defining moments at critical PowerPoint presentations, since these are all interesting to read about. In contrast, technological innovation often seems to come from hard work and good experiments, but this doesn't seem to make for an exciting story. So in general, a casual reader is left with the impression that the adoption of a technology is due mostly to inspired marketing and doesn't hear about hard technical work, unless it makes for a good copy, such as Bowerman's use of the waffle iron. Successful companies seem to have a fair share of both.

In 1979, Nike introduced a new way to cushion shoes: it sealed gas inside polyurethane capsules and embedded the capsules in the shoe's sole. The idea came from Frank Rudy, an aerospace engineer from North American Rockwell, who presented the idea to Nike in 1978. Prior to the use of air cushioning, running shoes used sponge rubber wedges for cushioning. The sponge rubber was relatively heavy and tended to compact over time. In contrast, the polyurethane capsules recover their original shape after impact and do not deteriorate over time as quickly as sponge rubber. One of the reasons that polyurethane capsules work is that the gas in the capsules contains large molecules, so that relatively little gas escapes from the capsules [105].

During the 26.2 miles of a marathon, a runner's shoes endure more than 25,000 impacts - the use of nylon uppers, waffle soles, and urethane capsules provides an important competitive advantage over traditional materials and construction. Nike began by targeting competitive racers, a relatively small and close knit community, which was receptive to these types of technical innovations. Moreover, Bill Bowerman's status and success as a coach increased the receptivity of the early adopters of these types of shoes.

During the same period of technological innovation, Nike had an equally impressive record of marketing achievements, including the following: in 1973, American record holder Steve Prefontaine was the first prominent athlete to wear Nike shoes. In 1977, the company began a marketing campaign with the tag line "There is no finish line." In 1978, BRS changed its name to Nike and tennis star John McEnroe was featured in Nike's marketing campaigns. In 1984 at the Los Angeles Olympics, Carl Lewis won four gold medals and Joan Benoit won the first women's marathon and both wore Nike shoes. In 1985, Chicago Bulls' Michael Jordan endorsed a line of AIR JORDAN shoes and apparel. In 1988, Nike began its "Just Do It" campaign. In 1992, the "Hare Jordan" Superbowl add featured Michael Jordan playing basket ball with Bugs Bunny [105].

These three forces — technology innovation, marketing innovation, and user receptivity — resulted in the sale of more than five million Nike Pegasus shoes, and are exactly the same forces that result in the acceptance of a new database or operating system.

4.5 Technology Roadmaps

> I don't know what technology will look like in twenty years, but if it is not in a laboratory today, then it is not a possibility.

Traditional

A *technology roadmap* is a series of concrete predictions by an individual or group about the evolution and trajectory of a technology. Technology roadmaps turn out to be quite handy due to the long time often required for basic research to reach end users in the market as new technology.

We begin by describing four important phases that most new technology goes through, beginning with basic research and ending with manufacturing and marketing.

Phase 1. Basic Research.   The first phase is scientific and consists of the discovery of new principles and phenomena. The goal of basic research is to improve our understanding of basic scientific and engineering principles, structures and mechanisms. A good example from the last chapter is packet switched communication networks that divide messages into packets and route the packets individually, instead of relying on a fixed circuit from the sender to the receiver as was previously done. Another example was the exploration of the basic properties of the elements Gallium and Arsensic and compounds synthesized from them prior to their use in integrated circuits. Today, most basic research is sponsored by the federal government and takes place at universities. Basic research is also done by a few of the largest companies, such as IBM and Microsoft.

Phase 2. Applied Research.   Applied research fleshes out the ideas discovered in basic research with the goal of developing new products and services. There is not a sharp division between basic and applied research. Today, there is a lot of research interest in understanding how a quantum computer might work. Most of this is basic research and focused on understanding the underlying principles of a quantum computer. Some very simple quantum devices have been built that can compute and store just a few quantum bits. Over time as the basic principles of building quantum computing devices are better understood, attention will shift to applied research focused on developing quantum devices that can store and compute with enough bits to be useful in practice. Applied research is done by researchers at universities and by research labs in large companies. In some industries — for example bioinformatics — applied research is also done by smaller companies.

Phase 3. Engineering Development. In the third phase, the ideas and principles discovered in basic and applied research are applied to build new devices and to deliver new services. After something new is discovered or understood, it can take quite some time to learn how to build it efficiently. In many fields, the main way of learning this is to build many wrong versions, until over time, someone eventually stumbles upon a correct version. As a simple example, it usually takes about a year to release a new version of a software product, and usually several versions before the product is mature enough that it is useful to a broad market. Here is a thought experiment to understand how difficult it can be to design and build a product (this only works for people over 40). Think about how many heavy suitcases you lugged through airports and compare that to how easy it is now to pull a suitcase with wheels through an airport today. Now try to understand why you never thought about adding wheels to suitcases. Engineering development is done by companies based upon basic and applied research done either in-house or by others. Small companies are particularly important here.

Phase 4. Manufacturing and Marketing. In the fourth phase, the products and services must be sold in large enough quantities and at good enough margins to create a successful commercial enterprise. Marketing is done by companies to help sell the products. Good marketing is quite hard. As we learned in the last chapter, marketing in general, whether good or bad, generally leads to clutter in the market. The products that companies market and sell can be either manufactured by themselves or outsourced to others to manufacture.

Here is an extreme simplification of these four phases: scientists discover things, applied scientists refine these dis-

coveries, engineers build things, and marketers explain to
people why they need things.

As a simple example of these four phases, consider the
development of the web server and web browser. The basic
computer science research underlying the browser included
advances supporting packet switched networks, distributed
computing, and related areas. As web servers and browsers
became widely deployed, applied research was undertaken
in a number of areas in order to develop more robust and
scalable web servers and web clients. For example, techniques were developed so that a single web site could share
its work load across dozens or hundreds of web servers.
By sharing the web load in this way, NASA web sites do
not crash when new images from Mars become available,
IRS web sites do not crash around April 15, and Victoria's Secret web sites do not crash when they stream online
webcasts.

The first browser, called Mosaic, was developed by a
small research group at the University of Illinois at Urbana-
Champaign. As the number of users began to grow, there
was commercial interest in browsers and engineering development was done by Netscape and Microsoft to produce
browsers with improved stability, performance and functionality. Finally, the "browser wars" between Netscape
and Microsoft were part of Phase 4, the marketing and
manufacturing of the browsers.

One of the better known technology roadmaps is the
yearly International Technology Roadmap for Semiconductors or ITRS. The 2005 ITRS roadmap contained over 200
tables of data and made thoughtful predictions about semiconductors 15 years into the future. The ITRS is sponsored by several semiconductor industry associations from
around the world and every two years identifies technology challenges and needs facing its members for the next
15 years. The 2001 ITRS roadmap was developed by over
800 experts from around the world organized into various
working groups and committees. For example, the 2001
roadmap predicted that microprocessors speeds will reach

over 10 GHZ by 2010 and memory chips will be 8 GB. It is important to note that it doesn't predict which vendors will still be in the business of producing and marketing memory chips in 2010. Table 4.5 contains some of the key findings from the 2001 ITRS.

4.6 Case Study: Clusters

A good example of the decades required to roll out a new technology is provided by what is called cluster computing. The basic idea is simple: lots of small commodity computers are linked together via a network to create a virtual supercomputer. With the commoditization of hardware and networking, this has become a cost effective way of creating supercomputers that are quite effective for certain tasks.

This idea is familiar to many from the SETI@home Project, which uses idle time on personal computers to search for extraterrestrial intelligence. The software to do this was made available in May, 1999. By July, 2002 over 3.8 million individuals had downloaded the software and donated some of the unused time on their computer to the project. With this strategy, the team was able to build one of the top ten most powerful supercomputers at the cost of a few servers and the cooperation of a few million personal computer owners who were interested in whether they are alone in the universe.

Here is another example. On January 8, 2003, a USA Today article with the title "High tech's latest bright idea: Shared computing" explained another application of this technology to the search for new drugs in this way:

> By day, Richard Vissa's PC sends e-mail, lets him surf the Web and handles other ordinary tasks. By night, when Vissa goes home, it becomes a super-powered computing machine, testing potential drugs for their ability to defeat disease. ... The company is one of many dabbling in a new technology that many in tech,

including IBM, say is one of the most promising new technologies in years. Dubbed shared computing, the technology allows companies to harness the processing power in every computer at all times and to combine it to crunch big computing tasks that before required expensive supercomputers.

There is a problem here, and it involves USA Today's use of the word "latest" in the phrase "high tech's latest bright idea." There is an implicit requirement imposed upon technology writers that they write articles about breakthrough ideas. This is because newspapers and magazines don't usually publish articles unless they involve a "breakthrough" or the "latest bright idea." This is despite the fact that all good technology writers know that technology can take years to be adopted by the marketplace. For example, more than eight years before the USA Today article, Business Week reported about a project that I was involved with using almost exactly the same words:

> Have a major problem that demands a supercomputer, but limited funds? ... Build a "virtual supercomputer" ... [by linking] a bunch of workstations...

In the 1993 grant proposal to the National Science Foundation to fund this project, a variety of prior and related research was cited stretching back to the late 1970's. There were two basic ideas: The first idea was that a bunch of computers in one location on a common local area network could work together on a common task. This is the idea of a cluster computing. Later, instead of a standard local area network, other more specialized techniques were also used to connect the computers and form a cluster.

The second idea was that geographically distributed computers from different administrative domains could also be linked together to create clusters of clusters or what were sometimes called meta-clusters. About five years later, in 1999, the idea of meta-clusters began to take off in a serious way as several supercomputing centers began to link their supercomputers together in what became known at that time as grids.

There were two types of clusters deployed. The first type were dedicated clusters that were devoted entirely to forming a virtual supercomputer. There were also clusters that used what was sometimes called "cycle stealing." With cycle stealing, computers could also be used for individuals for their standard work, and either at night when the computers were not being used, or at other times when the computers were idle, the computers would be incorporated automatically into the virtual supercomputer.

Several start ups tried to commercialize cluster computing in the early 1990's without much success. Several years later, in the late 1990's several companies tried to commercialize grid computing without much better luck. On the other hand, a company called Platform Computing that was around with related technology in the early 1990's has found a nice niche marketing cluster and grid technology, and, some of the larger companies such as IBM, Sun, and HP incorporate cluster and grid technology in their offerings.

More recently, cluster and grid computing have been reinvigorated by what is called cloud computing. With one type of cloud computing (sometimes called hosted clouds), clusters at the scale of data centers are operated by third parties, and computing is provided as a utility in the sense that you can get as little or as much as you need, and you pay for it by the slice. This greatly simplifies the delivery of cluster-based computing services and has made it easier for companies to adopt this technology.

Cloud computing was the cover story for the December 13, 2007 issue of Business Week and was described as "[as] a fundamental shift in how we handle information" [7], and in a later article by Business Week as "a major shift in the way companies obtain software and computing capacity [71]."

To summarize, the adoption of cluster computing by the marketplace took about two decades and went through several name changes and a few different business models. Throughout this process, vendors supplying cluster technology entered and left the marketplace. The adoption of cluster technology is fairly typical. It is usually quite difficult to predict *which vendors* supplying a technology will survive, but relatively easy to predict *which technologies* will survive.

4.7 Context

Context is one of the four basic forces introduced in Section 4.1 determining how long a new technology takes to reach Main Street (the "C" in RCMP). Context from this viewpoint includes three different but related aspects:

- Complexity. Some technologies are intrinsically more complex than others. Sending a message by email is simply not as complex as analyzing the digital data produced by a million customers and then using this analysis to improve a company's direct marketing. Also, the more complex a technology, the more decision makers in an organization are involved, and hence the more complex the sales cycle.

- Lock-in. Lock-in describes strategies employed by vendors to make it more difficult to switch to the technology offered by another vendor, as well as the implicit lock-in provided by a large base of users, who are generally reluctant to switch to another technology, even if it is better.

- Standards. Over the years, standards have played a more and more important role in the commoditization of technology. New technologies that leverage existing and emerging standards tend to be adopted more quickly.

In this section, we will describe each of the aspects of context in more detail, beginning with complexity.

Complexity. Perhaps the simplest way to think about complexity is that it is the underlying reason that so many technology projects fail. Here is my list of the top three ways in which complexity causes to technology projects to fail.

Reason 1 - It's is the people. The first reason is that a lot digital computing is simply too complicated for most people to use. Making the situation worse is the fact that most people who develop technology are pretty happy with the technology they develop, but pretty disappointed in the people who use it. The reason is that technology must be extremely well designed in order for people to use it effectively, and, unfortunately, most technology is not this well designed. Given the choice of blaming the technology or blaming the users, most developers find it much easier to blame the users and not to change the technology.

Reason 2 - It's the project. Deploying a new technology is a complex project. All complex projects are challenging for reasons having nothing to do with technology. Understanding this is as simple as thinking back to the last time you went to a large dinner party. Usually, there is a discussion about the problems someone is having remodeling their kitchen. The project is inevitably behind schedule. Moreover, there are always problems with the contractors and there are always surprises.

But think for a moment about this. Most people who remodel their kitchen have used an earlier kitchen for many years, have spent lots of time in other peoples' kitchens, have had many discussions with their friends about their friends' problems remodeling their kitchens, and then act surprised that their particular remodeling project is behind schedule, over budget, and likely to be disappointing when completed.

Compare this to a technical project. Many technical projects provide new capabilities and those running the

project often have little prior experience that is directly rel-
evant. At the same time, technology projects share all the
structural and organizational characteristics of any complex project, such as remodeling a kitchen. One should not
be surprised that technology projects end up behind schedule, over budget, and with disappointing outcomes, just like
remodeling a kitchen.

Reason 3 - It's the integration. Typically an IT system has
been built over a period of years, by a number of people,
through a large number of iterations. In general, no one
likes the system. The only thing it has going for it is that
it works. This is not to be underestimated. Its replacement
is likely not to work.

The reason it works is sometimes a bit subtle. Through
a series of iterations over years, the system gradually becomes better and better integrated with upstream systems
and processes that feed it and with downstream systems
and processes that it feeds. Say the system is one that
processes direct mail campaigns and that it was built ten
years ago. Assume that it takes an hour to prepare a campaign and the response rate of the campaign is 2.5% on
average. Assume that the new system promises to prepare
campaigns in 20 minutes and to get response rates of 3.0%.

The difficulty is the work required to integrate the new
system into the organization. The correct data must be fed
in, and the outputs must be integrated with the required
downstream systems. The prior work that integrated the
old system into the required upstream and downstream systems is likely to have been done by folks who have long ago
left the organization. The current staff often have not done
an integration like this before and are already behind schedule in other projects that are much less challenging and
threatening. The result is what you would expect: many
technology projects fail.

Lock-In or the Tyranny of Vendors and Users. One
of the more interesting battles in technology is the battle
between vendors to lock their customers into a technology

and thereby guarantee a long-term revenue stream, and their customers' desire to be able to switch vendors and technologies.

To phrase it more dramatically, the emergence of a new, and sometimes better, technology is thwarted by both the tyranny of the installed user base, who generally just want to be left alone, and the greed of the vendors, who are pursuing lock-in strategies designed to make it difficult for a user to switch a technology once it is deployed.

Once a technology reaches Main Street, it is usually so inexpensive that it lingers for quite a while, even if new technologies are much more efficient. For example, the Internet still has not eliminated the fax. As Odlyzko notes, "efficiency often plays a minor role when relatively inexpensive goods or services are involved [116]."

Contributing to lock-in is the cost of switching to a new technology, which can be very expensive. Here are some of the costs that may be involved:

- Search costs. Finding a new technology can often involve direct costs for searching for the technology. Most companies cannot switch to a new technology without a very large number of meetings. Just the coffee and donuts for the meetings begin to add up after a while. Complex projects usually involve pilot projects, which themselves can sometimes be expensive.

- Contractual commitments. Vendors try to negotiate long-term contracts. Getting out of a contract can be expensive.

- Capital costs. New technology can require new equipment. As a simple example, for many home users a new version of Microsoft Windows generally requires either a new computer or many free weekends and lots of coffee.

- Training. Learning new systems involves direct costs

for training and indirect costs for lost productivity during the transition period.

- Migrating data. Moving data from one format to another and from one system to another can be very expensive.

- Integrating new suppliers. Transition to new technologies sometimes requires new suppliers. Integrating new suppliers can sometimes be complex.

Standards and the Hope They Provide. When someone hears the word "standard" today, they often think of software standards such as HTML, HTTP, XML, etc. Standards, though, have always played a critical role in the adoption of new technology. A good way to understand the importance of information technology standards is to look at automotive standards and railroad standards.

The first Ford Model T was produced in 1908. Prior to that, cars were custom built by hand for the wealthy. In the first year of production, more than 10,000 model T's were sold for $950 each. In 1914, Ford sold more than 308,000 cars, which was more than the other 290 some automobile manufacturers combined. In 1915, he lowered the price to $280 and sold a million cars. The first Ford Model T took over 12 hours to assemble. By 1913, the time had been reduced to 1 hour and 33 minutes [19].

Ford introduced the production line to lower the cost of assembling cars. The Ford production line for the Model T consisted of a moving conveyor belt and different stations, where workmen repeated the same assembly task. This required parts which were precisely manufactured according to standards and were interchangeable.

To illustrate this approach, Henry M. Leland, the founder of Cadillac Motors, organized a demonstration of the British Royal Automobile Club in 1908. In the demonstration, three Cadillac cars were disassembled and the parts were mixed together. Then 89 parts were removed at random and replaced with parts from inventory. The cars were then were assembled and driven 500 miles without a problem [19].

The same basic ideas are at the root of the commoditization of the mainframe computer during the first era of computing and the PC during the second era of computing. Today, a PC can be assembled relatively easily by putting together standard motherboards, CPUs, disk drives, memory, and an operating system.

In contrast, the third era of computing is essentially controlled by communication standards, which can be viewed as broadly analogous to railroad standards. The gauge of a railroad is the distance between the inside faces of the two track. The most common gauge today is 4 feet 8 1/2 inches or 1435 millimeters, which was introduced sometime between 1822 and 1825 [24]. Without a standard, railroad service would be fragmented and limited to tracks of a single operating entity. The same is true of communication networks. The more networks that are interconnected, the more interesting and useful the network. This depends upon running a common set of communication protocols, such as the TCP/IP protocols described in Chapter 2.

The standards associated with the fourth era of computing are somewhat different and perhaps best thought of as broadly analogous to the Generally Accepted Accounting Practices (GAAP) used by accountants. In theory, two different accountants faced with the same books of a company and working independently and both following GAAP would come up with the same balance sheet, income statement, and cash flow statement. Of course, in practice this is not the case, but that is the goal. Web services are similar.

4.8   Case Study: Relational Databases

The technology adoption cycle can be seen quite clearly in the adoption of relational databases. A relational database is a software application that views data as a collection of rows and columns and provides mechanisms for creating tables of data, querying tables of data, and updating tables of data. Today the majority of business data is stored in relational databases, and, by and large, business are better off doing this than not doing this. The adoption of relational databases, though, was a process that took several decades.

At the beginning of the 1960's, many mainframe business applications could be viewed as processing data records by applying certain business rules. For example, a payroll application might read a record containing the number of hours an employee worked, read another record containing the hourly rate for the employee, read another record containing the employee's department, and use this information to prepare a check for the employee and address it to his department for delivery. The business rules would specify that the number of hours should be multiplied by the hourly rate to determine the gross payroll and then specify how to calculate the size of the deductions for federal taxes, state taxes, local taxes, health benefits, retirement deductions, etc. For large companies, this was a major advance over manual systems for payroll.

If an employee was promoted and moved to another department, one record containing the employee's hourly rate and one record containing the employee's department could be updated and the next payroll run would create a pay check with the correct salary and deliver it to the correct department.

As more and more payroll and similar back office systems were built, software engineers began to realize that the software code for working with records had certain common functions, including: 1) functions for creating tables; 2) functions for reading tables; 3) functions for updating tables; 4) functions for joining two tables together to produce a third table. These properties became the core of a relational database.

The conceptual framework for databases based upon tables containing data records and using joins to produce richer tables was described in a seminal paper by Edgar

(Ted) Codd with the title "A Relational Model of Data for Large Shared Data Banks," which appeared in 1970. Databases following the principles described in the paper became known as relational databases. Codd worked at IBM Research in Almaden, California at the time.

In the early 1970's, basic research and applied research was done in this area by two groups: the Ingres Project at Berkeley and the System R project at IBM. The Ingres Project resulted directly or indirectly in several commercial databases including Sybase's DBMS, Microsoft's SQL Server, Tandem's NonStop SQL, and Informix's DMBS. The System R project at IBM led to IBM's DB2 database.

Prior to relational databases, business data was stored either in custom applications or in what were called hierarchical or navigational databases. Querying these earlier types of databases required a skilled programmer, several lines of code, and knowledge of how the data was physically laid out on the disk. Later, relational databases came along with a language called SQL. Querying data could be done with a single statement in SQL.

The difference between navigational and relational databases can be thought of in the following way: with navigational databases you have to know where the data is in the same way that you have to know where the data is on your hard disk if you want to point and click through a sequence of folders to get there. With relational databases, you can access data by providing certain information to a database query in the same way that with a search engine you can access documents by providing key words to a search engine query. There is an important difference though: search engine queries are easy to write, while database queries are much harder to write.

Although writing SQL queries is complex, it is significantly easier than writing queries for hierarchical and navigational databases. In the 1990's, graphical front ends to relational databases became common, making it even easier for casual users to extract information from databases. Developing a query language with this type of power was one of the main motivations for the IBM researchers working on what became System R.

In the early 1980's, first generation vendors of relational databases included Ingres (a commercialization of the project at Berkeley), Sybase and Britton-Lee. The conventional wisdom of industry pundits was that relational databases were of interest to academics and useful for certain niche applications, but navigational databases, which were more scalable and had higher performance, were better suited for most serious commercial applications. Pundits recommended using an older technology called data dictionaries instead of relational databases as being the best way to integrate data into applications. During this period, twenty to thirty database transactions per second were possible on IBM 3084 processors [10]

By the beginning of the 1990's, twenty years after Codd's paper, the commercialization of relational databases was well along: relational databases could support hundreds of transactions per second and work with gigabytes of data. There were a variety of vendors providing relational databases including Oracle, IBM, and Sybase. Applied research began to shift to other topics, for example developing more specialized databases, such as databases for spatial data, image data, and scientific and engineering data.

In 2001, thirty years after Codd's paper, Yahoo replaced a proprietary home built system for assembling content such as headlines, stock charts and insider trading on its financial web pages, with MySQL, an open source relational database [75].

This case study illustrates some of the main themes in this book. First, the adoption of a new technology usually takes several decades. In this case, there was a span of almost thirty years between the first paper describing relational databases and their commoditization by open source relational databases such as MySQL. Second, among experts there was general agreement relatively quickly that relational database technology was an important core technology. Third, predicting which vendor of this technology would survive was beyond the pundits. Of the early vendors of database technology, only IBM has remained a significant market force. Fourth, in this span of thirty years, there has been plenty of clutter: There have been a few, but relatively few new ideas about relational databases, but there have been hundreds of academic papers about them, and thousands of more popular articles.

4.9 The Pain and Pleasure of Technology

A good technology salesperson always tries to understand the difficulties or, in sales jargon, the pain that potential customers feel. This is one of the topics discussed in this section and is the "P" in RCMP. To ease pain caused by current technology is one of the main reasons people buy new technology.

Trying to understand why people buy technology may seem hard. During the year you are reading this, there will be millions of decisions made resulting in the purchase of technology. In principle, each individual is unique and each decision to purchase is unique; therefore, it would seem that predicting the adoption rate of new technology would be difficult.

In actual fact, probably the opposite is true, and people purchase new technology for only a handful of reasons:

As a toy. Toys bring pleasure and people like pleasure. Many decision-makers in technical positions are particularly susceptible to the pleasure of buying and playing with new technology. It is often the reason that they worked so hard to get and to keep their job. The more secure their position, the more likely they are to tell themselves that it is their *responsibility* to try new technology. It is their duty.

To spend a budget. New projects have budgets and budgets get spent. Technology gets bought whether it is

needed or not and whether it works or not. One of the
interesting consequences of the Internet bubble was the following. Many new companies were formed and new capital
was infused. New projects got started and technology got
bought. The pace was such that often when visiting a start-
up you would look around and see software costing tens of
thousands of dollars that hadn't even been taken out of
the box. After the Internet bubble, budgets grew tighter
and it was rare to see unopened software around. On the
other hand, the same philosophy can often be seen today in
marketing budgets. Marketing budgets are designed to be
spent, regardless of whether the company has the discipline
to measure accurately the return on the dollars spent. Of
course it is not always easy to measure the return of marketing dollars: there is a fair amount of truth in the adage
that half an advertising budget is just wasted - the problem
is you never know which half.

To ease pain. In most situations when someone is in pain,
your response is one of sympathy. Not so in technical sales
when pain indicates an opportunity. Pain in this situation means something is not getting done and someone is
in trouble. For example, customers are complaining that
x doesn't work. Or the sales manager doesn't know how
many widgets are getting sold and who is buying them. Or
the CEO doesn't have nice colorful reports about sales by
region and by product to pass to the board who will file
them with only a glance. The role of a technology company is to create products and services which, in the ideal
world, result in the easing of these types of pain.

The early market is dominated by decision-makers who
primarily buy technology for the pleasure it creates. One
of the mysterious facts about the world, which perhaps is
best not to think too deeply about, is that occasionally
new technology works beyond all expectations, and provides a fundamental advantage to those using it. What this
means is that, from time to time, adopters of technology in
the early market gain a fundamental competitive advantage

over their competitors by deploying a new technology.

This is very similar to winning the lottery. Although only one person wins a lottery, the word spreads extremely quickly and everyone who has bought a ticket feels that his or her purchase is justified. The organization running the lottery is highly motivated to spread the word. The media picks up the story since their audience is anxious to hear this type of story, in order to justify their purchases of tickets.

Technology success stories in the early market are the same. Stories about the (rare) successes of new technology in early markets are widely reported since the technology media realize that this is exactly the type of stories their readers want.

Before we end the section, it is useful to describe two other reasons people make purchases.

To gain a competitive advantage. Well disciplined organizations purchase technology to gain a competitive advantage. Although you would expect this to be a common reason, there are several reasons it is not. First, it is difficult to choose the right time to deploy new technology. The earlier a new technology is chosen, the more likely it is to lead to competitive advantage (since your competitors have not yet adopted it), but the more likely it is to fail (since the technology is still immature). Since it is difficult at most organizations to be associated with projects that may fail, in general managers push out the adoption of technology until it is quite likely to succeed, but less likely to lead to a competitive advantage.

As an aside, most arguments justifying competitive advantage use quadrant diagrams (see Figure 4.1 for an example). For those who haven't used them, this is how a quadrant argument goes. The "good" quadrant is the upper right and with the right technology a company can move from one of the "bad" quadrants to the upper right. Unfortunately, the technology usually doesn't understand that this is why it was being deployed and often does not

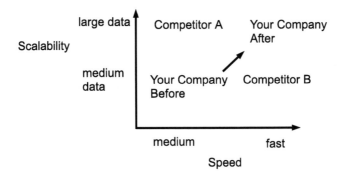

Figure 4.1: The argument for moving to a new technology as prepared by the Director of Marketing of a high tech company. After the technology is deployed, the company will be in the upper right quadrant, the place all high tech companies want to be. One of the jobs of the marketing department is to select two dimensions (speed and scalability in this example) so that the company ends up in the upper right quadrant.

immediately drive the company to the upper right hand quadrant. As a consequence, project managers deploying new technology sometime become demoralized.

As a source of hope. At the beginning of every January, fitness centers are always full and overflowing. By the beginning of February, they are back to their normal levels. The reason is hope. And this is a good reason. For the same reason, many nice, fancy workout clothes are bought each year over the holidays and most are worn only once or twice. Technology is bought for the same reason. Much of it is never installed. Hope is good though. Without hope, we would all go back to paper and pencil.

In the end, people make technology purchases and start technology projects for reasons that are usually not as rational as they may seem at first. Marketers know this and design campaigns exploiting this.

Product	Number of Years
Telephones	20
Television	15
Cable Television	10
Cell Phones - Nokia	5
Personal Computers - IBM	< 3
Internet - AOL	< 3

Table 4.4: This table shows the number of years that various technologies took to reach Main Street. It is important to note that most companies never reach Main Street. This is illustrative of the more general phenomenon that while predicting breakthroughs is extremely difficult, identifying breakthroughs is much easier, as is predicting their trajectories, including when they will reach Main Street. On the other hand, predicting which particular vendors will reach Main Street is quite hard, and perhaps best modeled as a random walk. The table is somewhat misleading: in some sense, most of these technologies took about 10-20 years to reach Main Street when viewed from the perspective of the entire technology road map from laboratory to end user. On the other hand, the time for a particular vendor to reach 1 Million end users depends very strongly on when they entered the market. For example, AOL reached a million users less than 3 years after it was started in 1985; on the other hand, that was over 13 years after the first email was sent in 1972.

	2001	**2005**	**2010**	**2016**
DRAM Half-Pitch (nanometers)	130	80	45	22
DRAM Memory Size (megabits or gigabits)	512M	2G	8G	64G
DRAM Cost/Bit (microcents)	7.7	1.9	0.34	0.042
Microprocessor Physical Gate Length (nanometers)	65	32	18	9
Microprocessor Speeds (MHz)	1,684	5,173	11,511	28,751

Table 4.5: This table contains some technology predictions made by the International Technology Roadmap of Semiconductors (ITRS) in 2001. They predicted that by 2010 the cost of DRAM memory will decline to 1/20 of the cost in 2001 and microprocessors will be 10 times faster. By 2016, the cost of DRAM memory will be less than 1/100 of the cost in 2001 and microprocessors will be 15 times faster.

Year	Event
1961	Charles Bachman at the General Electric Company develops the Integrated Data Store (IDS), an early database.
1967	The CODASYL Database Task Group (DBTG) begins work on the Network Database Model.
1968	IBM introduces a database called IMS running on IBM System/360's. IMS uses a navigational data model, but is not compliant with CODASYL data models being developed at the time.
1970	IBM's E. F. Codd publishes the first paper describing relational data models.
1971	The Conference on Data Systems Languages (CODASYL) releases its first standards report. CODASYL products are developed by Eckert-Mauchly Computer Corporation, Honywell Incorporated, Siemens AG, Digital Equipment Corporation (DEC), and Prime Computer Corporation.
1973	Another prototype relational database project called Project Ingres is started at Berkeley.
1974	IBM develops a relational database called System R during 1974–1975. An improved version is developed and tested during 1978–1979. System R uses the query language SQL, which eventually becomes an industry standard.
1980	IBM releases SQL/DS, a relational database for mainframe computers.
1980's	Ingres Corporation, Britton-Lee and Sybase commercialize the technology developed by the Ingres and System R projects.
1983	ANSI/SPARC survey finds over 100 relational database implementations.
2002	The open source MySQL database has an estimated 4,000,000 active installations worldwide, with up to 27,000 downloads per day.

Table 4.6: The adoption of the relational database by businesses took several decades and generated a lot of market clutter. This table is adopted from [99] and [37].

4.10   Case Study: Adoption of Linux

This case study is about the adoption of an operating system called Linux and begins in 1991, when a Finnish student named Linus Torvalds wrote the following email message asking readers of the newsgroup comp.os.miunx what features they would like to see in a new free operating system.

```
From: torvalds@klaava.Helsinki.FI (Linus Benedict Torvalds)
Newsgroups: comp.os.minix
Subject: What would you like to see most in minix?
Summary: small poll for my new operating system
Message-ID: <1991Aug25.205708.9541@klaava.Helsinki.FI>
Date: 25 Aug 91 20:57:08 GMT
Organization: University of Helsinki

Hello everybody out there using minix - I'm doing
a (free) operating system (just a hobby, won't be
big and professional like gnu) for 386(486) AT
clones. This has been brewing since April, and
is starting to get ready. I'd like any feedback
on things people like/dislike in minix, as my OS
resembles it somewhat (same physical layout of
the file-system (due to practical reasons) among
other things).

I've currently ported bash(1.08) and gcc(1.40), and
things seem to work. This implies that I'll get
something practical within a few months, and I'd
like to know what features most people would want.
Any suggestions are welcome, but I won't promise
I'll implement them :-)

Linus (torvalds@kruuna.helsinki.fi)

PS. Yes - it's free of any minix code, and it has a
multi-threaded fs.  It is NOT protable [sic] (uses
386 task switching etc), and it probably never will
support anything other than AT-harddisks, as that's
all I have :-(.
```

Year	Version	Est. Number Users	Est. SLOC
1991	0.01	100	10,000
1992	0.96	1000	40,000
1993	0.99	20,000	100,000
1994	1.0	100,000	170,000
1995	1.2	500,000	250,000
1996	2.0	1,500,000	400,000
1997	2.1	3,500,000	800,000
1998	2.1.110	7,500,000	1,500,000
2000	RedHat 6.2	NA	1,500,000/17,000,000
2001	RedHat 7.1	NA	2,400,000/30,000,000

Table 4.7: The early growth of Linux. The estimate for the number of lines of source code for period 1991-1998 are for the entire distribution, while the estimates for 2000 and 2001 are for only the Linux kernel, as well as for the entire distribution. Sources: [86], [156], and [157].

The first release of Linux was in 1991 and within five years there were over 1,000,000 users.

This is amazing for several reasons. The first release of Linux was written by a student and later versions (to this day) are written by a community of volunteers. Linux is an example of what today is usually called open source software, since the operating system (and its source code) can be downloaded free of charge. Linux was able to reach 1,000,000 end users and Main Street in less than five years despite some significant disadvantages: 1) it competed against operating systems developed and maintained by professional engineers working at Microsoft and Sun Microsystems; 2) it had essentially no marketing budget and could not hire expensive consultants to help it reach Main Street; and 3) several vendors launched campaigns to discredit it and open source software in general.

The Mythical Man-Month. A good question to ask is why does the open source software movement works at all? Although most open source software projects involve just a few programmers, larger ones, such as the development of Linux, involve hundreds of programmers, all of whom are volunteering. Any large software project is quite challenging; until the success of Linux, few people would have predicted that a software project as complex as the development of an operating system could be completed by a team of volunteers.

The basic problem is a fundamental one: adding more programmers typically slows down large projects. This is because adding three times as many programmers produces three times as much code but usually creates more than three times as many interfaces in the code, and interfaces are often associated with software bugs.

Here is a simple example to explain the basic issue (in practice the issue is not quite this simple). Assume that each day, a programmer produces 500 lines of code containing 5 functions of 100 lines each. Assume that the 5 functions developed by that programmer work well together. But now, that programmer may find herself using the five functions of a second programmer, as well as five functions of a third programmer to complete certain tasks. This produces five times five times five or 125 combinations to check for errors, possibly subtle ones.

In this sense, although the amount of code increases linearly with the number of programmers, the number of interfaces, and hence places for possible bugs, grows geometrically. This is a well recognized problem and was explained carefully over twenty years ago in a class book called the Mythical Man-Month [Brooks:1995].

The term "mythical man-month" comes from the following observation. It is tempting to estimate project sizes as follows. Estimate the number of lines of code in the final project. Divide by the number of lines that each software engineer can code each month to get the number of person-months required. This almost never works since doubling the number of software engineers can easily *increase* the amount of time required to complete the project for the reason above.

Successful open source projects share a number of characteristics, including some of the following:

- **Successful open source projects typically contain small, well designed cores.** The small core is written by just a few programmers, perhaps one, and the rest of the system, perhaps millions of lines, interfaces to it with simple, well-defined interfaces. Of course, this approach is often also used by companies that develop software.

- **Open source software is often written by professional programmers.** Although open source software can be obtained without charge, open source software is often written by professional software engineers. This occurs for several reasons: first, professional software engineers like writing code and especially like writing code that is elegant, important, and widely used. The right open source projects give them an opportunity to do this. Second, some companies today have business models that charge for services that are based in part upon open source software. For example, a database consultant can charge for setting up and maintaining a complex database that is built using the open source database MySQL and the open source web application development system PHP. If the success of his project requires helping fix a bug in MySQL or developing a small extension to PHP, then he is often happy to help.

- **Extensive testing.** Software is buggy. There is no way around this. The benefit of open source development is that there are large number of software engineers available to test and debug the code on a wide variety of systems in a wide variety of configurations. Bugs get identified quickly and fixed quickly.

Chapter 5

The Era of Data

5.1 Introduction

Big Data is a Big Deal

Tom Kalil, White House Office of Science and Technology
Policy, March 29, 2012

The world's total yearly production of print, film, optical,
and magnetic content would require roughly 1.5 billion
gigabytes of storage. This is the equivalent of 250
megabytes per person for each man, woman, and child on
earth.

Peter Lyman and Hal R. Varian, How Much Information,
2000

This chapter is about the fifth era of computing — the
era of data. For a quick overview of the first four eras of
computing, see Table 1.2 in Chapter 1. Since we are just
beginning the fourth era of computing, the era of devices,
writing about the next era with any specificity is not so
easy.

161

5.2   Thinking about Big Data

Digital data is measured in bytes. A byte is enough storage to store a number in the range 0 – 255. A kilobyte (KB) is a thousand bytes, a megabyte (MB) is a million bytes, and a gigabyte (GB) is a billion bytes. A single page of text (without any graphics or images) can be stored in a few KB, a MP3 song in a few MB, and a DVD quality movie in a few GB.

A terabyte (TB) is a trillion bytes and this is a good unit to think about text information. A terabyte is the same thing as one thousand gigabytes or one million megabytes or one billion kilobytes. Around 2000, a study that we will discuss in more detail in the next section, estimated that all printed material available comprised approximately 200,000 terabytes. At that time, terabyte sized datasets were rare.

Thinking about terabytes takes a little bit of practice. A single page of plain ASCII text is about 2–3 kilobytes, but we rarely see plain ASCII text anymore. The same amount of text in Microsoft Word is about 100 KB. Adding a few images can increase the size to a few MB. On the other hand, scanning a page can reduce this to about 50 KB.

Assuming that a four drawer file cabinet contains enough space for about 10,000 pages and that each page requires about 50KB to store it, means that two file cabinets can hold about 1 GB of data, while 2,000 file cabinets can hold about 1 TB of data.

For many years, large corporations have managed thousands of file cabinets. On the other hand, until about a decade ago, spinning a TB of disk was expensive and the software required to manage it was primitive. For example in 1994, a TB of disk cost about one million dollars. By Johnson's law this has decreased dramatically over the past decade. In 2003, a TB of disk cost about $3000, in 2008, it cost $250, and in 2011, you could buy a 2 TB disk for $100.

On the other hand, just because our laptops now store terabytes of data does not mean we have a good understanding of how to manage, search, explore, or analyze that much data.

Over the past decade or so, datasets that are terabyte size or larger have become common. This is partly due to the fact that over the past decade text data has become a smaller and smaller fraction of the digital data that is produced each year. Billions of sensors and other digital devices (think of phones that constantly broadcast where they are) now produce streams of data, and thousands of different scientific instruments produce terabyte size datasets on a daily basis. Digital data is everywhere, and people can easily carry terabytes of data in their pockets. We entering the era of big data.

Today, talking about big data requires units larger than terabytes. A petabyte (PB) is one thousand terabytes; an exabyte (EB) is one million terabytes; and a zettabyte (ZB) is billion terabytes.

In 2009, Marissa Mayer, who was the Vice President for Search Products & User Experience at Google gave a talk at Xerox PARC in Palo Alto California and she estimated that in 2002 there were about 5 exabytes of data online. She also estimated that this had grown to about 282 exabytes by 2009, the time of her talk.

When thinking about big data, I have found the following rule of thumb to be helpful: The amount of data that big data facilities manage increases by a factor of approximately 1000 per decade as Table 5.1 shows. Also, the total amount of online data is probably approximately 1000 times larger than that. This rule of thumb has held true for the last twenty years or so.

For example, in 1996 I worked on a big data project that spun a few terabytes of disk, which was a very large amount then. The amount of online data was estimated to be measured in petabytes at that time. A little over a decade later, big data facilities managed petabytes of data and Mayer estimated the amount of online data in the world in the hundreds of exabytes. If we assume that growth will continue at approximately this rate, then over the next decade, big

Data in big data facilities	
Period	**Amount**
1990–2000	Terabytes
2000–2010	Petabytes
2010–2020	Exabytes

World wide production of data	
Period	**Amount**
1990–2000	Petabytes
2000–2010	Exabytes
2010–2020	Zettabytes

Table 5.1: The amount of data managed by big data facilities and the approximate amount of online data in the world.

data facilities will manage exabytes of data and the world wide production of data will be measured in zetabytes.

In practice, engineers managing big data today no longer speak in terms of terabytes and petabytes. Instead they speak in terms of megawatts (MW). For example, an engineer might say that she works at a 15 MW data center that manages hundreds of petabytes of data.

5.3 The Commoditization of Data

The amount of new data produced each year is rapidly growing, but estimating exactly how much new data is produced each year is not straightforward. A good analysis was done by a research group led by Peter Lyman and Hal Varian at the School of Information Management and Systems at the University of California at Berkeley in 2000 [81]. Although outdated now, it is still very informative. The study clearly showed that by 2000 data was becoming commoditized.

Interestingly, the study was supported by EMC, a ven-

Scale	Examples	Comments
Kilobytes (1955–1965)	Econometric models	Computerized econometric models work with kilobytes of data.
Megabytes (1965–1985)	US Census	Individual records from the US Census are aggregated into data files which are megabytes in size.
Gigabytes (1990–2000)	Human genome	The human genome is about 4 gigabytes.
Terabytes (1995–2015)	Sloan Digital Sky Survey	Scientific instruments can produce terabytes of data. For example, the Sloan Digital Sky Survey (data release 1) was a 2.5 terabyte size atlas of the sky.
Petabytes (2005-2025)	Climate simulations	Numerical simulations of global warming can produce petabytes of data.

Table 5.2: This table shows the approximate size of a data set that could be analyzed using the technology from the five different eras of computing that are described in Chapter 1. As the table shows, the scale of the data we can store, analyze, and use as a basis for discovery and decision support has increased by a factor of over a trillion in less than fifty years.

dor of storage solutions. Table 5.3 summarizes some of their estimates for the amount of new data produced around the time the report was written.

Here are some of the conclusions from their study [81]:

- Between 1,000,000 and 2,000,000 terabytes of new information was generated in 1999.

- This information was stored primarily on print, film, magnetic, and optical media. The majority was stored on hard disks (a magnetic media).

- The majority of new data is born digital these days and not in analog format (such as print and film).

- Approximately three times as much new information (or between 3,000,000–6,000,000 terabytes of data) consists of information flows and streams through electronic channels such as telephones, instant messaging, radio, and TV.

We close this section with two important remarks.

First, it is important to note that Table 5.3 assumes the data is compressed. For example, the study estimates that somewhere between 1 TB and 8 TB are required to store in a digital format all the new books that are published each year. Approximately a million books are published each year [81]. Scanning the books at 600 dots per inch yields about 40 MB per book, which can be compressed to about 8 MB, and which represents approximately 1 MB of text. This gives an estimate of 40 TB of scanned data, 8 TB of compressed data, and 1 TB of text data. Viewed from another perspective, in the year 2000 when the study was published, you could build a digital library for your home office consisting of twelve 80 GB disks, requiring less space than a small boombox, and costing less than $3000, that could store the text for all the books published that year. Of course, by the time you read this, as a consequence of Johnson's law, the cost will be much less.

Storage Medium	Type of Content	TB/Year, Upper Estimate	TB/Year, Lower Estimate	Growth Rate, percent
Paper	Books	8	1	2
	Newspapers	25	2	-2
	Periodicals	12	1	2
	Office documents	195	19	2
	Subtotal:	240	23	2
Film	Photographs	410,000	41,000	5
	Cinema	16	16	3
	X-Rays	17,200	17,200	2
	Subtotal:	427,216	58,216	4
Optical	Music CDs	58	6	3
	Data CDs	3	3	2
	DVDs	22	22	100
	Subtotal:	83	31	70
Magnetic	Camcorder Tape	300,000	300,000	5
	PC Disk Drives	766,000	7,660	100
	Departmental Servers	460,000	161,000	100
	Enterprise Servers	167,000	108,550	100
	Subtotal:	1,693,000	577,210	55
Total		2,120,539	635,480	50

Table 5.3: This table contain estimates of the worldwide production of original content in 1999 that is stored digitally, measured in terabytes. The assumption is that the data is compressed. Source: Peter Lyman and Hal R. Varian, How Much Information, 2000.

Second, the transition from analog data (such as analog photographs) to digital data (such as digital photographs) comes with certain trade-offs.

In 2006, Nikon, one of the leading manufacturers of film cameras for the past few decades, announced that it would stop manufacturing most of its film cameras and instead concentrate on manufacturing digital cameras [108]. Not everyone is happy with this transition: analog film generally has higher resolution and analog cameras can last for decades, while for many owners, it is a challenge to keep a digital camera working for two years. On the other hand, digital photographs are very easy to share with others by email and to publish on the web.

An important open question though is how many digital images taken today will be around in 20 years. Taking photographs using an analog camera, printing them on high quality paper, and storing then in a shoe box was a very safe way to preserve photographs for decades. Taking photographs using a digital camera, publishing them on a web site, and storing them on your home PC, may not be a safe way to preserve photographs for even five years.

5.4   The Data Gap

Unfortunately, although the amount of data produced each year is *growing* very rapidly, the number of people who have the proper training to analyze this data is essentially *constant*. For example, as Table 5.4 shows, the number of new Ph.D.'s who graduate each has been essentially constant. What this means is that there is a growing gap — the *data gap* between the amount of data available and our collective ability to analyze it.

There are only three possibilities:

1. We ignore more and more data. In large part, this is what is taking place.

2. We develop new technologies to automate in part our

ability to analyze data and extract useful information from it. To some degree, this is in fact taking place.

3. We have no problem, because the people who analyze data are much smarter and more efficient than they were ten years ago. Some of my friends who analyze data tell me that this is the case and that therefore their salaries should be about 10–1000 times higher than they were ten years ago to keep pace with their new abilities. Other people I know are more skeptical.

One of the fundamental challenges for the Fifth Era of Computing is to reduce this data gap. For perhaps the first time in human history, data is now becoming a commodity. It joins hardware cycles, computer software, and network bandwidth as a component of our technical infrastructure that has been commoditized.

To put this into some perspective, Darwin spent 17 years collecting one of the data sets for his monograph *Origin of the Species*. This data set consisted of a few hundred observations (KB of data). In practice the data was available only to him and his close collaborators and had to be copied by hand. Today, a scientist can access Gigabytes of other scientists' data within minutes, even if that data is located half way around the world. Viewed from one perspective, scientists today can access data sets that are at least 1,000,000 times larger (GB vs KB), in time frames that are at least 10,000 times faster (in the 19th century a messenger on a horse would require approximately 20 days or 28,800 minutes to travel a thousand miles vs just a few minutes to transfer a GB of data today over a high performance network). From this perspective, one is tempted to either raise one's opinion of scientists in the 19th century or to lower one's opinion of scientists in the 21th century.

Although we are no longer starved for data, the problem today is that we lack the tools and technologies that would enable us to extract useful information from even a small fraction of the available data.

Year	Number New Ph.Ds
1990	22,868
1991	24,023
1992	24,675
1993	25,443
1994	26,205
1995	26,536
1996	27,241
1997	27,232
1998	27,278
1999	25,933
2000	25,966
2001	25,548
2002	24,588
2003	25,289
2004	26,275

Table 5.4: The total number of new Ph.Ds in science and engineering awarded in the US each year. The number is essentially constant, and yet the amount of new data produced each year is growing exponentially. This gap means that most data today is being ignored. Source: US National Science Foundation, Division of Science Resources Studies, Survey of Earned Doctorates [103].

We close this section by looking at the commoditization of data from another perspective, which is the emergence of community and personal digital libraries that contain in an easily accessible digital format significant portions of all the information that our civilization has ever produced.

For example, Google is partnering with Harvard University, Oxford University, Stanford University, the University of Michigan and the New York Public Library to build a digital library containing scanned images of all the books in their holdings.

As another example, as the table below shows, for less than one thousand dollars, an individual can put together a personal digital library consisting of several hard disks that can store enough books, images, and audio recordings for a lifetime, and enough video recordings to fill a few hours of each day.

What this means is that, if so inclined, for the first time in human history, an individual can carry the Bible, the works of Shakespeare, classic Greek literature, and thousands of other works of literature and art on a memory stick about the size of your key chain that can easily fit into your pocket or get lost in your purse.

These are all examples of the commoditization of data and information. There is no reason to expect that the impact will be any less than the impact of the commoditization of time in the 18th century or the commoditization of processing power in the 20th century.

To summarize, in the Data Era, data is a commodity, but extracting useful information from the data is a bottleneck.

5.5   Extracting Knowledge from Data

The goal of statistics is insight, not computation.

Traditional

A mathematician, a physicist, and an engineer were
traveling through Scotland when they saw a black sheep
through the window of the train. "Aha," says the
engineer, "I see that Scottish sheep are black." "Hmm,"
says the physicist, "You mean that some Scottish sheep
are black." "No," says the mathematician, "All we know
is that there is at least one sheep in Scotland, and that at
least one side of that one sheep is black!"

Traditional

For most of us, data is not an end in itself, but rather a
mechanism to gain knowledge about the world around us.
From the perspective of science, knowledge about the world
comes from only a handful of mechanisms:

- *Theory.* Arguably, the oldest way that we have gained
  knowledge about the world has been through theoretical insights. A theory in this context refers to knowledge gained by starting with axioms and definitions
  and proving theorems. One of the best examples of
  this type of knowledge are the propositions and theorems in Euclid's Elements. For example, Proposition
  6 of Book 1 states: "If in a triangle two angles equal
  one another, then the sides opposite the equal angles
  also equal one another." This is just as true now as
  when it was written over 2000 years ago.

- *Experiment.* An important change took place with
  the scientific revolution that occurred in the 17th century. From this time forward, knowledge gained from
  experiments became the basis for our understanding
  of the world. For example, Galileo's experimental

observations of the positions of the planets began a process that eventually replaced the Ptolemaic view of the world, in which the planets orbited the earth, with the Copernican view, in which the planets orbit the sun.

- *Simulation.* The idea of simulation is that complex physical processes can be simulated on computers and knowledge can be gained by an analysis of these simulations. One of the early uses of this technology occurred in the Manhattan Project during World War II when the mathematicians Stanislaw Ulam and Nicolas Metropolis used the technique to study nuclear fission. An important contemporary use of simulation is to study global warming. Since surface temperature records only go back about 150 years, and since society is producing carbon dioxide and other gases in unprecedented amounts, simulation is a very important tool to study the impact of these gases on future surface temperatures.

- *Data Mining.* Today, the large amounts of data that are available from repositories, databases, and other sources, enable *new* knowledge to be created directly by looking for patterns in already collected data, without having to do new experiments or simulations. For example, GenBank is a publicly available online database maintained by the US National Institute of Health [8]. In 2008, it contained over 85 billion nucleotide base pairs from over 260,000 different organisms and was doubling in size approximately every 14 months. Discoveries can be made by the analysis of this data and by comparing this data to other public and private databases. There is no agreed upon name yet for obtaining knowledge in this way; in addition to the term data mining, the terms knowledge discovery from databases (KDD) and data-driven (DDD) discovery are also used.

Note that the last two mechanisms are both quite recent, while the experimental method is only several hundred years old.

Theory. Pythagoras made the discovery that some numbers are fundamentally different than other numbers in the sense that they couldn't be represented either by integers or by the ratio of two integers.

Today, we use the term *rational numbers* to include these two types of numbers; that, is, numbers that are either integers or the number formed when one integer is divided by another integer, such as 1/2 or 1/3. If a number is not rational, it is called *irrational*.

Another basic property of numbers concerns divisors. Some numbers have no divisors other than 1 and and the number itself. They are called *prime numbers*. For example, 2, 3, 5, 7, 11, etc. are prime numbers. Any other number can be written as a product of primes. For example, $12 = 2 \times 2 \times 3$. It turns out that every number can be written as a product of primes, and that this is unique except for the order of the primes. In this example, although 12 can be written in three different ways as the product of primes ($12 = 2 \times 2 \times 3 = 2 \times 3 \times 2 = 3 \times 2 \times 2$), in each case, the prime 2 occurs twice and the prime 3 occurs once.

If we assume that *every number can be written as a product of primes and that this representation is unique except for the order of the primes*, then a short argument (called a *proof*) shows that the square root of two is irrational. The argument requires only a paragraph and can be found in the notes to this chapter.

Knowledge obtained in this way is a good example of theoretical knowledge. Although we may have to read the proof several times (or many times) in order to understand it, once we we understand it, we are usually pretty confident of its truth.

According to legend, Pythagoras was quite disturbed by this theoretical discovery that some numbers were irrational. The Greeks at the time of Pythagoras viewed numbers geometrically, as the length of line segments. Using a straight edge, a line could be drawn. Using a compass, equal units could be marked out along the line. These correspond to the natural numbers: 1, 2, 3, etc. Fractions arose naturally by examining geometric figures and corresponded to the ratios of two line segments. For example, 1/2, 1/3, 3/5, and 7/4 arise in this way. However, a square whose sides are of length 1 has a diagonal which can be constructed geometrically using a straight edge and a compass, but whose length doesn't correspond to the ratio of any natural numbers, as the argument above shows. No wonder Pythagoras was disturbed. Today, our approach would probably be to outlaw straight edges, since we are careful to protect our children and to keep them from being disturbed by uncomfortable facts.

Experiment. In 1609, Galileo invented a telescope which could magnify distant objects by a factor of about 20×. He turned it to the heavens and began to observe and measure. He immediately observed that Jupiter had four moons, that the moon had mountains, just like Earth, and that there were large numbers of stars that could not be seen with the naked eye. He quickly published a pamphlet called *Sidereus Nuncius,* or the *Starry Messenger* .

With telescopes, it was now much easier to measure the orbits of the planets, both the *fixed* stars which "orbited" the Earth once a day, and the so-called *wandering* stars (planets), such as Mercury, Venus, Mars, Jupiter, and Saturn. With these measurements, the theory that the Earth revolved around the sun, which had been advanced by Copernicus, half a century earlier, suddenly took on a new urgency.

Simulation. The paper "The Monte Carlo Method" by Metropolis and Ulam was published in 1949 in the Journal of the American Statistical Association and explains how simulation can be used to study complex physical processes.

The mathematicians Stanislaw Ulam and John von Neumann introduced the term during the Manhattan Project for the computer code that simulated nuclear fission. The basic idea is to use random numbers to simulate and approximate complex physical processes. According to [61], the name "Monte Carlo Method" was due to Ulam. Ulam had a relative who loved to gamble in Monte Carlo, which is the capital of Monaco.

The complex simulations that required supercomputers in the 1980s can now be done easily using personal computers. For example, several different companies now offer Monte Carlo simulations to help with retirement planning [45].

Here is a simple example of how Monte Carlo algorithms can be used in retirement planning from [45]. Consider a recent retiree with $200,000 invested in the Standard & Poor's 500-stock index with the goal of using the proceeds over a 20 year period. Since the S&P has had an average return of about 14% since 1952, one answer is to withdraw $32,000 each year.

The problem is that a 14% average return means that some years have a higher return and some years have a lower return. If there were to be a string of bad years early in retirement that resembled the stock market in the mid 1970s, then withdrawing $32,000 a year would use up all the money in eight years. Monte Carlo simulations can compute the likelihood of this and related scenarios.

Data mining.   On June 26, 2000, there was a joint press announcement in which the public Human Genome Project and the private Celera Corporation jointly announced the completion of a working draft of the human genome after roughly 10 years of work [110]. The map of approximately 30,000–35,000 human genes and approximately 3 billion DNA base pairs is publicly available. (By the way, a few years later in 2004, the number of genes was reduced to about 20,000-25,000.) Fundamental discoveries can now be made by using techniques from data mining to analyze this data and by comparing it to other public and private databases.

Item	Storage Required	Comments
Book	1 MB	The 20 million books in The Library of Congress require about 20 TB to digitize as ASCII text. If the books are scanned, then about 10 times more storage would be required.
Low Resolution Image	20 KB	There are about 52 billion photographs taken each year, requiring about 520 PB to store.
Medium Resolution Image	1-10 MB	The Library of Congress has about 13 million images which would require about 13 TB to archive at 1 MB/image. High resolution images might require up to 130 TB at 10 MB/image.
MP3 audio files	1 MB/minute	80 years of listening requires about 42 TB of disk.
DVD video files	2 GB/hour	Four hours of video per day for ten years requires about 16 TB, which is not enough video for most teenagers.

Table 5.5: A 1 TB disk can be purchased today (in 2011) for less than $100. It is likely that by 2015, you will be able to purchase a 800 TB disk for the same amount. This would hold enough books, images and audio files for a lifetime, but not quite enough video. The information in this table is adapted from [57].

5.6   Case Study: The Orbit of Mars, Kepler's Law and Brahe's Data

Many of the simple facts we take for granted today rest upon data that is not so easy to collect and not so easy to understand. In this section we consider a simple yet instructive case study illustrating this observation. Today, many school children know that the planets revolve around the sun (it turns out that not all school children know this), and many of these know that the orbit of a planet, such as Mars, is an ellipse with the Sun at one of the foci.

It turns out, though, that determining the orbit of Mars from visual observations is not straightforward (it was not until 1610 that Galileo published the The Starry Messenger describing some of the first observations of Mars using a telescope). From the viewpoint of predicting the orbits of the planets, the Ptolemaic system is very good. The Ptolemaic tables were based on the assumption that the sun and planets moved in orbits which consisted of small circles. The centers of these small circles traced out larger circles whose center was the earth. More precisely, the model consisted of large circles called *deferents* that circled the earth. The planets moved in small circles called *epicycles* whose centers followed the deferents. Finally, the earth was not at the center of the deferent, but rather displaced from it. This approach allowed very accurate prediction of the motion of the sun and the planets. With this system, the orbit of a planet around the earth is determined by the following three parameters: the diameter of the deferent, the diameter of the epicycle, and the displacement of the earth from the center of the deferent.

Tycho Brahe (1546–1601) spent most of his life making visual observations of the stars and planets. The data he collected was some of the most accurate data collected without a telescope. Brahe fitted a model of the solar system to this data. In this model, i) the earth was at the center; ii) the sun revolved around the earth in a circle;

and, iii) the planets revolved around the sun in circles. It turns out that this model fitted his data very well.

In fact, both Brahe's model and the Ptolemaic model fitted Brahe's data better than heliocentric model of Nicolaus Copernicus (1473–1543), in which the sun is at the center and the planets revolve around the sun in circles. So much for the simple stories we learned in school as children.

This kind of situation occurs quite often when working with data. Complex models that do not reflect the underlying physical phenomena accurately (such as Ptolemy's model, consisting of deferents and epicycles, or Brahe's model, in which the sun circles the earth and the planets circle the sun) may yield more accurate predictions than simpler models (such as the Copernican heliocentric model, which captures the basic fact that the planets orbit the sun).

Let's call this phenomenon *Ptolemaic convenience* — often the most accurate statistical model available misrepresents basic properties of the underlying physical phenomenon it is modeling.

Over time, our understanding of the models that reflect the correct underlying physical phenomena grow and these models become more accurate (and sometimes more complex).

For example, it was not until 1609 that Johannas Kepler (1571–1630) developed an accurate heliocentric model. One of Kepler's fundamental insights was that the planetary motion was not based upon circles but upon ellipses. With this insight, Kepler produced the first heliocentric model that was as accurate as Ptolemy's geocentric model.

Note that ellipses require only two parameters to specify their shape (the diameter of the major and minor axes). In other words, Kepler's model used one fewer parameters to fit each orbit than Ptolemy's and was equally accurate. In data analysis, this is sometimes called *Occam's razor*: there is a strong preference for the statistical model with the fewest parameters that fits the data.

Later, Isaac Newton (1643–1727) showed that elliptical orbits are a consequence of the inverse square law of gravitation. This provided additional evidence for Kepler's heliocentric model.

This tension between Ptolemaic convenience, model driven insight, and Occam's razor occurs in many different areas. As a simple example, think of how we model consumer behavior today. The most accurate models for whether a consumer will respond to an offer to purchase a product or pay a bill on time are statistical, data-driven models that represent Ptolemaic convenience and have little or no relation to phenomena that actually drive consumer behavior. They are used today simply because they work, which was exactly the same reason that Ptolemaic models were used for centuries to predict planetary motion. Predicting consumer behavior using models that try to mirror the underlying psychological processes present is so inaccurate that it is not a serious option for anyone trying to predict the actual behavior of consumers.

Developer	Description	Accuracy
Ptolemy (83-161)	Earth at center of the universe. Planets and stars revolve in small circular orbits called epicycles, whose centers orbit the Earth in much larger circular orbits.	fits observations very accurately
Nicolaus Copernicus (1473-1543)	Sun at center of universe. Earth and other planets revolve in circular orbits around Sun. This model explained the retrograde motion of the sun without requiring epicycles.	Copernican model did not fit observational data as well as Ptolemaic model.
Tycho Brahe (1546-1601)	Earth at center of solar system. Sun revolves around earth; planets revolve around sun in circular epicyclic orbits.	Brahe's data fits his observational data very well, but has the sun orbiting the earth.
Johannas Kepler (1571-1630)	Sun at center of solar system. Planets revolve in elliptical orbits, with the sun at one of the ellipse's foci.	Kepler's model fits Brahe's observational data very well and is much simpler than Brahe's or Ptolemy's models.
Isaac Newton (1643-1727)	Newton showed that Kepler's model follows from the inverse square law for gravitation.	Experimental data from the telescope fitted Kepler's model better.

Table 5.6: Accurately predicting the motion of planets and stars was critical both for both producing calendars and for navigating.

5.7   Pearson's Law

> The value of a column of data grows as the square of the
> number of columns it is compared to.
>
> Pearson's Law

A particularly simple form of data is regular and rectangular. Data like this can be thought of as being organized
into tables, with each table consisting of rows and columns
of data, and with a separate table for each source of data.
Given data like this, we can ask the question, what additional insight into the data do we gain as we add additional
data sources containing additional columns of data?

It is the experience of many people that the knowledge
we gain from data grows quickly as we add new attributes
(if the data is regular and rectangular, attributes are simply
new columns of data). If we are optimistic, then we can
hope that as we add more columns of information, then
our insight into the data grows as the square of the number
of columns. There is no standard name for this law, so we
call it Pearson's Law, after the statistician Karl Pearson,
who lived from 1857–1936.

Pearson's law is not meant to be understood literally,
but rather more metaphorically, in the same way that Metcalfe's law was first formulated by George Gilder. For convenience, we repeat here Gilder's description of Metcalfe's
Law, which we discussed in Chapter 1.

> In this era of networking, [Robert Metcalfe] is
> the author of what I will call Metcalfe's law of
> the telecosm, showing the magic of interconnec-
> tions: connect any number, "n," of machines -
> whether computers, phones or even cars - and
> you get "n" squared potential value. Think of
> phones without networks or cars without roads.
> Conversely, imagine the benefits of linking up
> tens of millions of computers and sense the ex-
> ponential power of the telecosm.

George Gilder, Metcalf's Law and Legacy, Forbes
ASAP, September 13, 1993.

Here is an example of Pearson's Law. A study published
in 2000 noted that there is a relation between El Nino and
the outbreak of cholera [121]. More precisely, there is a correlation between the El Nino-Southern Oscillation (ENSO),
a measure of the sea surface temperature anomalies off the
coast of South America, with the outbreak of cholera in
Africa. Both the outbreak of cholera and El Nino have
been studied extensively, but by comparing their respec-
tive oscillations over time, it appeared that the the two
oscillations were related. Further investigation showed the
El Nino events increased the temperature of certain areas
of the sea surface. This increase in temperature resulted
in increased numbers of the Vibrio cholerae bacteria that
cause cholera and that live among the zooplankton in the
ocean.

Here is an another example of Pearson's Law. Consider
the following data about Florida voters during the 2000
Presidential campaign. There are 67 counties in Florida.
In this campaign, Buchanan was a Reform candidate who
received an unusually large number of votes in Palm Beach.
The ballot in Palm Beach county was a butterfly ballot that
many voters found difficult to decipher. From one database,
you can obtain the number of registered Reform voters by
county. The first table below contains the number of voters
by county who were registered as Reform party members
for the 2000 Presidential election. The second table below contains the number of votes by county for Buchanan.
If you think of county as a link or a key, you can combine the information in the first two tables to produce the
third table. One way to understand the information in this
third table is graph it. Let the horizontal axis represent the
number of registered Reform voters and let the vertical axis
represent the votes for Buchanan. Once this is done, Palm
Beach immediately stands out, suggesting the possibility
of something unusual occurring in Palm Beach. This is a

good example showing that columns of data become more interesting as they are compared to other columns of data.

County	Registered Reform Voters
Alachua	91
Baker	4
Bay	55
Bradford	3
Brevard	148
Broward	332
Calhoun	2
etc.	etc.
Palm Beach	337
etc.	etc.

County	Votes for Buchanan
Alachua	263
Baker	73
Bay	248
Bradford	65
Brevard	570
Broward	788
Calhoun	90
etc.	etc.
Palm Beach	3407
etc.	etc.

Table 5.7: These tables contain data from the 2000 Presidential election in Florida. The top table contains the number of Reform voters registered to vote in the 2000 Presidential election in Florida by county. The middle table the number of votes for Buchanan in the 2000 Presidential election in Florida by county.

County	Registered Reform Voters	Votes for Buchanan
Alachua	91	263
Baker	4	73
Bay	55	248
Bradford	3	65
Brevard	148	570
Broward	332	788
Calhoun	2	90
etc.	etc.	etc.
Palm Beach	337	3407
etc.	etc.	etc.

Table 5.8:   The table above is the result of joining the previous two tables using county as the key or link. Note that Palm Beach stands out.

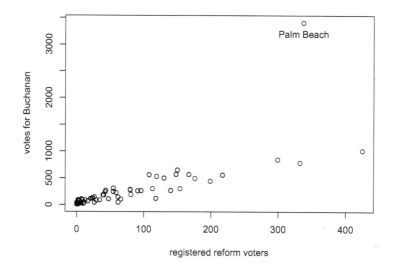

Figure 5.1: Data from the 2000 Presidential election in
Florida. This graph shows the result of comparing one column of data, the number of registered Reform voters, with
another column of data, the number of votes for Buchanan.
The two columns are merged by using county as the common key. Note that Palm Beach stands out.

5.8   Data Just Wants to Be Free: The Bermuda Principles

Lawrence Lessig, a professor of law at the Stanford Law School, has argued very persuasively about the opportunities that will be lost as intellectual property laws put more and more restrictions on digital content [79].

Lessig distinguishes between *controlled* resources and *free* resources. A basic example of a controlled resource is private property. The owner of private property has well established rights to control who has access to the property. A basic example of a free resource is a highway: access to highways is open and uniform. If there are fees to use the highway, then they are applied uniformly and consistently and no one can be restricted from using the highway.

The Internet started as a resource whose content was basically free in this sense. Over time, more and more of the content has become controlled.

Data is a very specific, but very important, type of digital content. There is often quite an important benefit to the public when data is freely available. An interesting example is provided by research that is funded by the U.S. Government. The results of research funded by the U.S. Government are generally required to be made available to the public. On the other hand, the Bayh-Doyle Act encourages universities to commercialize government funded research. A mechanism for commercializing research is to restrict the results of research to those who provide licensing revenues. A common practice today is to balance these two requirements by making data that is "close to the science" publicly available without limitation, while patenting processes that are "close to the market" and can lead directly to an income stream through licensing.

We have discussed open source software in Chapter 2 and some of the mechanisms that have been introduced to formalize open source software, such as the various open source software licenses. Interest is growing these days in providing a similar framework for data so that it is open and freely usable by any interested party. Sometimes this is called *open data*.

The Human Genome Project was started in October, 1990 with the goals of a) sequencing the approximately 3 billion DNA base pairs that comprise the human genome and b) identifying what, at the beginning of the project, was estimated to be about 30,000 to 35,000 genes in this sequence. (By the end of the project, it turned out that there were fewer than 20,000 genes, but that each gene could code multiple proteins in a much richer and more varied fashion than originally thought.)

At the beginning of the project a fundamental decision was reached that the Human Genome Project, and similar projects that were funded by the U.S. Government, had to make the genes and sequences that were discovered freely available to the public. The rules for making genomic data publicly available are sometimes known as the Bermuda Principles, after a meeting in 1996 that was held in Bermuda [35]. Today, an online database called GenBank contains this data and can be freely queried by anyone in the world. A simple example is below, where show the first 40 base pairs in the human gene TBC1:


```
acaatattgt gcagcccaca gatatcgagg aaaatcgaac
```


The data from GenBank is freely used by scientists from universities and companies throughout the world and has significantly sped up the pace of bioinformatics research and discovery. If the GenBank sequence data had been restricted, many of the analyses that biologists use daily would be quite different.

For example, a scientist who identifies a new gene in a rat will use GenBank and a program called BLAST to search for similar genes in the human.

5.9　Case Study: The World Population

Some of the complexities of working with data quickly become apparent if we think a bit about something as basic as the world population. Suppose you are interested in the question of how the world population has grown over time. As a point of reference, the world population in 2010 was about 6.8 Billion [142].

Data from Table 5.9 is from the U.S. Census Bureau, which has brought together some data to answer this question [142]. The table contains data from several sources and estimates the world's population beginning in 10,000 BC (between 1 million and 10 million) and ending in 1950 (between 2.4 billion and 2.5 billion). For simplicity, Table 5.9 contains a summary and data from a single source (Biraben) and ends in 1800. The full table, has nine other sources.

Data doesn't get much simpler than this, but already there is some complexity and some irregularity in the data. The first irregularity comes from missing values. For example, if the data is thought of providing lower and upper estimates for world population, then the upper limits are missing for the years 4000 BC to 400 BC. Although a note on the web site explains that for these years, the lower limit should be used, the table itself contains missing values for the upper estimates.

The second type of irregularity comes from the fact of how the upper and lower population limits are computed. For some years, there is only a single number, for some years two numbers, for other years three numbers, and for some years ten numbers. Presumably, the more numbers, the more reliable the estimates. Notice that the upper and lower limits are just one way to summarize the variation of several estimates. Another is to use a measure of how close together or how spread out the various estimates are.

A third type of irregularity comes from the fact that

the intervals between the estimated dates vary from year
to year. Again, this is not a problem for a table as small as
this, but as the size of the table grows, this can introduce
subtleties in how other estimates are produced using data
in this table.

These irregularities are straightforward to recognize when
the data is analyzed by a human. On the other hand, in
the Era of Data, more and more data is analyzed by machines using automatic processes. In this case, these types
of irregularities can sometimes lead to problems when data
that was collected for one purpose at one time is used for
another purpose at some other time.

| Year | Summary | | Biraben |
	Lower	Upper	
10000 BC	1	10	
8000 BC	5		
6500 BC	5	10	
5000 BC	5	20	
4000 BC	7		
3000 BC	14		
2000 BC	27		
1000 BC	50		
500 BC	100		
400 BC	162		162
200 BC	150	231	231
1	170	400	255
200	190	256	256
400	190	206	206
500	190	206	206
600	200	206	206
700	207	210	207
800	220	224	224
900	226	240	226
1000	254	345	254
1100	301	320	301
1200	360	450	400
1250	400	416	416
1300	360	432	432
1340	443		443
1400	350	374	374
1500	425	540	460
1600	545	579	579
1650	470	545	
1700	600	679	679
1750	629	961	770
1800	813	1,125	954

Table 5.9: The table above shows historical estimates of the world population. All numbers are in millions. Source: U.S. Census Bureau.

5.10   The Shape of Data

It is sometimes helpful to think of data in terms of its shape. In this section, we will describe five of the basic shapes that data commonly takes: tables, trees, sequences, event streams, and graphs.

Tables. Perhaps the most familiar type of data is a table. Tabular data consists of rows representing data records and columns representing data attributes. For example, a company might keep a table of its employees containing the employee number, first name, last name, date of birth and date of hire. In another table, it might keep a table of its employees' current addresses, containing employee number, street address, city, state, zip, and the date that the address was updated.

Dividing data into different tables like this is common. Here is an example of why organizing data this way is useful. In a corporate database, the data for many different applications may have the need for an employee address. There are two options: either this information can be entered explicitly in each table using one or more columns or this information can linked to each of these tables using an employee number. In the latter case, when the employee moves, only one table needs to be updated.

Databases are designed to optimize the accessing and updating of data records, which are rows in the table. On the other hand, applications for data analysis are designed to optimize the analysis of columns of data. When data is stored on disk it must be stored either by row so that database operations are fast or by column so that statistical operations are fast. This is because data is moved from disk to the processing units in chunks called blocks and whatever data is transferred in a block can be easily processed together for greater efficiency.

Trees. Another shape that data can take is called semi-structured. A good way to visualize semi-structured data is as a tree. For example, statistical models are sometimes ex-

pressed in XML, which is one of the languages that is used
to describe semi-structured data. Figure 5.2 contains a part
of XML description of a statistical model that classifies an
iris into one of three types based upon the length and width
of its petal and sepal. XML contains structures called elements that are enclosed in tags. For example in Figure 5.2,
the first element is called PMML. The element is bracketed
by the two tags <PMML> and </PMML>. Similarly,
the element PMML contains two other elements: DataDictionary and Classification Model. This structure continues
and both DataDictionary and Classification Model contain
other elements, giving this data the structure of a tree.

Sequence Data.   Although sequence data has been
around for some time, its importance has grown recently as
the Human Genome Project made large amounts of genome
sequence data publicly available. Here is an example of a
sequence from the human gene TBC1, which we have already seen above:

```
acaatattgt gcagcccaca gatatcgagg aaaatcgaac
tatgctcttc acgattggcc agtctgaagt ttacctcatc
agtcctgaca ccaaaaaaat ...
```

This is a sequence of length 100 built from the four
letters "a", "c", "t" and "u," called bases, which represent the four amino acids Adenine, Cytosine, Guanine and
Thymine. The sequence data in the human genome consists
of a sequence just like this but of length 3 billion instead of
length 100. Given another sequence, say 1000 bases from
the genome of a mouse, a typical question a molecular bi-
ologist might ask about this data is: "Does the sequence
match, either exactly or approximately, a sequence of the
same length, in the human genome?" Sequence data has
the shape of a line in a long row of old fashioned printer's
type. Think of it this way. When a printer sets type, the
printer chooses a letter from a pile of letters and then set
the letter into a line or slug of metal type. Sequence data

```
<PMML version="2.0">
 <DataDictionary numberOfFields="5">
  <DataField name="PETALLENGTH" optype="continuous"/>
  <DataField name="PETALWIDTH" optype="continuous"/>
  <DataField name="SEPALLENGTH" optype="continuous"/>
  <DataField name="SEPALWIDTH" optype="continuous"/>
  <DataField name="SPECIES" optype="categorical">
   <Value value="setosa"/>
   <Value value="versicolor"/>
   <Value value="virginica"/>
  </DataField>
 </DataDictionary>
 <ClassificationModel functionName="classification">
  <MiningSchema>
   <MiningField name="PETALLENGTH" usageType="active"/>
   <MiningField name="PETALWIDTH" usageType="active"/>
   <MiningField name="SEPALLENGTH" usageType="supplementary"/>
   <MiningField name="SEPALWIDTH" usageType="supplementary"/>
   <MiningField name="SPECIES" usageType="predicted"/>
  </MiningSchema>
  <Node score="setosa" recordCount="150">
   <ScoreDistribution value="setosa" recordCount="50"/>
   <ScoreDistribution value="versicolor" recordCount="50"/>
   <ScoreDistribution value="virginica" recordCount="50"/>
   <Node score="setosa" recordCount="50">
    <SimplePredicate field="PETALLENGTH" operator="lessThan"
      value="24.5"/>
    <ScoreDistribution value="setosa" recordCount="50"/>
    <ScoreDistribution value="versicolor" recordCount="0"/>
    <ScoreDistribution value="virginica" recordCount="0"/>
   </Node>
                  . . .
  </Node>
  </Node>
 </ClassificationModel>
</PMML>
```

Figure 5.2: This figure contains some semi-structured data
that describes (a fragment) of a statistical model for clas-
sifying an Iris into threetypes: Iris setosa, Iris versicoloar
and Iris virginica.

has the same shape: what matters is the letter chosen and the order of the letters in the line.

Event Streams. Another simple data shape consists of a stream of events and an associated collection of entities. Perhaps the most familiar example of event and entity data consists of credit card transactions. A merchant selling goods or services who accepts credit cards sees a stream of credit card transactions that identify the purchases each day. On the other hand, each credit card transaction has a unique account number identifying the cardholder. Over time, by looking at all the transactions associated with a specific account number, the merchant can assemble a picture of the types of goods or services that the cardholder purchases. Similarly, the bank that issued the credit card can analyze all of the credit card transactions of the cardholder and assemble a picture of the cardholder's purchasing behavior.

Some additional examples of events and entities are in the table below, and we will discuss this type of data in more detail in a later section.

Event-entity streams can be thought of as two related tables. To see this, think of an event stream of credit card transactions. In this case, the first table is a table consisting of the credit card transactions. Think of these as sorted by time. Each row contains, for example, the time and date of the transaction, the amount, the name and location of the merchant, and the name and account number of the card holder. The second table in this case is a table with one row for each account number that summarizes the various purchases made by that card holder. For example, the columns in this second table might include: the total number of transactions in the past 30 days, the total dollars spent in the past 30 days, the total number of transactions in the past 90 days, the total dollars spent in the past 90 days, the total number of purchases at restaurants in the past 90 days, the total dollars spent at restaurants in the past 90 days, etc. With enough features like these, a fairly

	Event	**Entity**
credit cards	credit card transaction	credit card account
frequent shopper cards	purchases	shopper
telephone calls	call detail record	telephone number
air plane tickets	passenger name record	passenger
online browsing	viewing a web page	Internet user

Table 5.10: This tables contains some common examples of event-entity streams.

good statistical characterization of the cardholder can be generated.

Notice that this statistical characterization doesn't require using the name, address, or any other information that could identify the cardholder. All that is required is a mechanism for grouping together credit card transactions that belong to the same person. There are several ways of doing this that do not require using personal information.

Graphs. You can think of a graph as a diagram that consists of nodes, viewed as small circles, and edges, viewed as lines that connect the nodes. The web is a familiar example of data that can be viewed as a graph. Think of each web page as a node and connect two nodes with an edge in case there is a hyperlink from the first page to the second. With powerful enough web crawlers, you could compute a graph like this, consisting, say of 8 billion nodes and 20 billion edges.

Independent of the content of a page, the graph defined above can provide some interesting information about the importance of a page. For example, the more links to a page, the more authoritative you might expect the page to be. Google was the first commercial search engine to

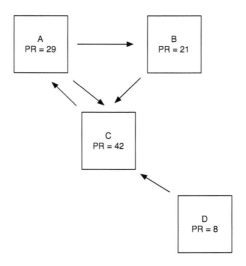

Figure 5.3: This figure shows a simple graph containing four nodes and five edges. Each node also shows its page rank (abbreviated PR). The notes for this section give the formulas for computing the page rank.

use page links in this way to help order the results of a search. This ordering is now called the Google Page Rank and plays an important role in the quality of the Google search engine.

As a simple example in the figure below, the web page C has three incoming links, while the pages A and B each having one incoming link, and the web page D has no incoming links. In this simple example, the page ranks would be A - 29, B - 21, C - 42, and D - 8. If two or more pages contain the same search terms, then the pages with higher rank would be presented first.

5.11   Case Study: Consumer Databases

In 1970, the US Congress passed the Fair Credit Reporting Act (FCRA), which led to the consolidation of the credit reporting industry and the emergence of three national credit bureaus: TransUnion, Experian, and Equifax. Today, each of these maintains data on approximately 190 million Americans. The data is refreshed daily from hundreds of different sources and used for a variety of purposes, including the following:

- Credit data is used to compute scores that qualify consumers for new credit cards. Credit card issuers use these scores to create direct mail lists of prospects for new credit cards. These days, once you have a job and a credit card with a good payment record, it is rare for a week to go by without seeing a few of these offers in the mail.

- Consumer credit data is used to provide "instant credit," enabling you to qualify for an automobile loan and to drive away with a new car minutes after you make the decision to buy the car.

- Consumer credit data is also used to determine the likelihood that you will default on a home mortgage. This information is used by companies underwriting mortgages to determine whether to offer you a mortgage and, if so, at what interest rate.

Today we take the wide availability of credit cards, the existence of instant credit, and the ability to refinance our homes easily for granted, but prior to the emergence of national credit bureaus, obtaining credit was not so easy. An offer of credit was handled locally and credit decisions were done manually. For example, the decision of whether to offer you credit would be done by a credit officer at a local bank, who was often less likely to offer credit if you were new to town or somehow perceived as untrustworthy.

An offer of credit was often quite subjective. Today, an
offer of credit is based upon data collected by the three
major credit bureaus and dictated by scores. The higher
the scores the more credit you will be offered and the less
it will cost.

In order to compute credit scores, credit bureaus collect
and maintain a wide variety of information about individuals, their transactions, and their public records, including:

- **Personally Identifying Information.** This information is sometimes known by its initials (PII) and
  includes your name, phone number, date of birth, social security number, current address, previous addresses, current employer, and previous employers.
  Personally identifying information is extracted from
  a variety of sources, including the credit applications
  you fill out.

- **Trade and Account Information.** For each account that involves an extension of credit, the credit
  bureau maintains a variety of information, including
  the account type, the name of the company providing
  the credit, the account number, the date the account
  was opened, the current balance, the credit limit or
  loan amount, the monthly payment, and the payment
  pattern during the past few years. The account type
  indicates whether the account is an installment loan,
  such as an automobile loan with a fixed monthly payment, or a revolving line of credit, such as a credit
  card account whose monthly payment varies. The
  trade and account information is provided by companies that you do business with, including credit card
  companies (e.g. CitiBank, MBNA), retail companies
  with a credit card (e.g. Gap, Land's End, etc.), banks
  and other institutions providing loans (e.g. mortgages
  and automobile loans).

- **Public Records.** Credit bureaus also collect a variety of public records, including bankruptcy records,

monetary judgments entered against you, and tax liens from state and county taxing authorities.

- **Requests for Credit Reports.** A credit report also includes a list of companies that requested your credit report.

- **Credit Scores.** A credit score is often attached to a credit report. One of the most popular credit scores is provided by the Fair Isaac Corporation and commonly called the FICO Score. The FICO Score ranges from 300 to 850, with higher numbers indicating greater credit worthiness.

As with almost all new technologies, there are trade-offs. First, any system collecting such a large amount of information is bound to include a certain amount of inaccurate data. Getting inaccurate data out of the system can be quite a challenge. Second, any system used by so many different businesses for so many different purposes is likely to attract a certain amount of fraud and related misuses. Third, after a while, there is a tendency for "mission creep" to take place: although credit bureaus exist to allow business to make offers of credit, they can be used by law enforcement agencies to help with investigations, by state agencies to identify deadbeat parents, and by the Transportation Security Administration to identify potentially dangerous travelers.

As with most technology trade-offs, a simple rule holds: as long as the negative aspects of a new technology affect other people, the technology is good; as soon as the negative aspects begin to touch me or the people I love, the technology is bad.

To understand this trade-off better, let's look at numbers for one type of bad event: using stolen identities to obtain credit cards fraudulently. This is an example of identity theft that occurs when criminals use your personal information, such as your name, date of birth, or social security number to obtain goods, services, or credit in a fraud-

ulent manner. For example, in 2005 there were 255,565
identify theft reports made to the U.S. Federal Trade Commission, and about 30% of these involve a fraudulent use
of a credit card.

From one perspective, over 250,000 cases of identify
theft is a very big problem. From another perspective, it is
what those in the world of credit refer to as "just the cost of
doing business." For example, with over 480 million credit
cards used in the U.S., these cases of fraud mean that each
year about 6 out of 10,000 credit cardholders are affected,
which is much less than 1 percent.

Understanding this type of risk is usually quite personal:
it is considered small if during the past year, you have used
your credit card, refinanced your home, or purchased a new
car using instant credit without a problem; it is considered
a travesty if during the past year, you or someone in your
family has been the subject of a identity theft.

Looking at the trade-off from another point of view,
between 1970 and 2002 the percentage of people in the U.S.
with credit cards has grown from 16 percent to 73 percent,
the cost of credit has declined, and the ease of obtaining
credit has increased dramatically. For those people with
good credit scores, credit at low interest rates is readily
obtainable; while for those with poorer credit scores, credit
is generally obtainable, but is more costly. In contrast,
prior to 1970, it was difficult even for those with good credit
histories to shop for good credit rates, while those with poor
credit histories could generally not obtain credit. Today,
with credit bureau data available online to retailers and
vendors, one can obtain credit information so quickly that
credit scores are used for some Internet transactions.

In the fifth era of data, these types of trade-offs will
become more and more common. More and more third
parties will collect more and more data about more and
more people and their transactions. As long as the vast
majority of people benefit, most people will probably feel
comfortable with the trade-off between benefit and risk,
despite the corresponding loss of privacy. On the other

	2000	2001	2002	2003
Identity Theft Complaints	31,117	86,198	161,819	215,177
Fraud Complaints	107,890	133,891	218,284	327,479
Total	139,007	220,089	380,103	542,656

	2004	2005	2006
Identity Theft Complaints	246,882	255,613	246,035
Fraud Complaints	410,709	437,906	428,319
Total	659,595	695,524	676,360

Table 5.11: Identity theft and fraud complaints reported to the US Federal Trade Commission Consumer Sentinel system. Part of the increase from year to year is due to the growing awareness and use of the system. Source: Federal Trade Commission.

hand, by the very nature of the system, there will be more and more opportunities for misuse and correcting data will become more and more difficult.

5.12   Creating Digital Data

The easiest way to think about digital data is that it is anything that is comprised of bits and that fills up a hard disk. Originally, computers were primarily used for scientific computation and digital data consisted mainly of numerical data that was generated by mathematical computations running on the computers.

Later, as businesses began to use computers also, the type of digital data computers worked with began to change. Companies were primarily interested in working with data about their customers, suppliers, and internal business processes. Digital data was created either manually, such as when a new employee was hired and the employee's address and salary were manually entered, or a memo or email was written and sent out, or automatically, such as when a pay-roll was paid by the payroll system and various records were generated.

More recently, the type of digital data that computers work with has changed again as consumers have begun to use computers. Today, more and more digital data is being generated by consumer devices, such as .mp3 files contain-ing music that has been ripped from a CD, JPEG images produced by digital cameras, and MPEG-4 video files pro-duced by digital video recorders.

Once data is in a digital format, it becomes much eas-ier to manipulate it and to study it. For example, people have been studying the bible ever since it was first writ-ten. A concordance, which shows for each word each of its occurrences, is often useful when carefully studying a text. Until very recently, creating a concordance has been a monumental work.

Once a text has been digitized, however, concordances can be created with a very simple program. For example, a very basic concordance for Genesis can be created on a lap-top today with a program of less than a hundred lines that takes a fraction of a second to run. One quickly finds that Genesis has 38,277 words and that a concordance contains 2588 words. Processing the text more carefully will take a bit longer, but even so, a clean concordance can be ob-tained in less than a minute of computation using a laptop computer.

Working with text data in English is relatively easy, be-cause of the simple encoding used: for example, the ASCII encoding uses 0-127 to represent the 26 letters in the al-phabet and other standard characters such as a line feed or space. In ASCII, a space is coded as 32, a period is coded as 46, A is coded as 65, B is coded as 66, C is coded as 67, etc.

The process by which speech is converted into a digital format is worth considering. The first step is creating an alphabet and rules for converting speech into words formed from the alphabet. Although this may seem obvious, think

| A Simple Taste Alphabet ||
Taste	Coding
salty	1
sweet	2
sour	3
bitter	4

Table 5.12: A simple encoding of tastes.

| Another Taste Alphabet ||
Sensation	Coding
salty	1
sweet	2
sour	3
bitter	4
umami	5
astringent	6
pungent	7

Table 5.13: A more complex encoding of tastes.

about how you would create an alphabet for a language with which you are not familiar, such as Chinese, or how you would create an alphabet for another sense, such as pictures that you see, sensations that you feel, or scents that you smell.

Another example is provided by odors. The Yale OdorDB contains 140 different odors. Imagine building an odor coder that monitors odors in a room and once a second producers a vector containing 140 numbers (an "odor vector"), with the first component in the vector measuring the concentration of the first odor, the second component measuring the concentration of the second odor, etc. Similarly, imagine that you wanted to fill a room with a particular odor. In this case, one could build an odor decoder that given an odor vector would release the appropriate amounts

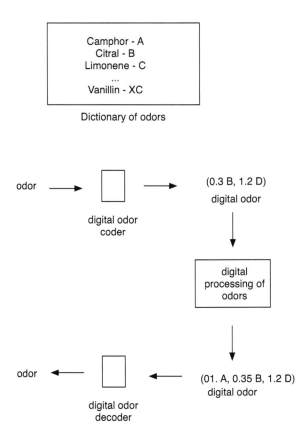

Figure 5.4: This diagram shows how odors might be digitally encoded.

of each of the 140 different odors. It would contain 140 different small vials, just as a color printer contains 4 colors.

Once an alphabet is available, it is a simple matter to encode the alphabet in a digital format, such as ASCII for text, JPEG for images, etc.

Once the data is stored digitally, the next step is to analyze and transform it in different ways using a program. For example, a digital concordance simply counts and indexes all the words in a text document.

To summarize, creating and working with digital data usually involves the following basic steps:

1. Defining the symbols - The first step is to define a collection of symbols (an alphabet) and rules for creating more complex structures from the symbols. For example, text is created from letters that form an alphabet, and words are defined by a sequence of letters. As another example, a pixel is created from symbols coding red, green and blue (RGB) values, while an image is created from a two-dimensional grid of pixels.

2. Encoding - taking an analog signal and creating digital data out of it using the different words in the dictionary.

3. Processing - processing the digital data using a variety of programs and processes.

5.13   Using Data to Make Decisions

Solving a problem simply means representing it so as to make the solution transparent.

Herbert A. Simon, The Sciences of the Artificial

There are two possible outcomes: If the result confirms the hypothesis, then you've made a measurement. If the result is contrary to the hypothesis, then you've made a discovery.

Attributed to Enrico Fermi

People have various relationships with data. Broadly speaking, you can divide these relationships into three groups. The first group is the largest and consists of people who have a perfectly natural tendency to either ignore data or to run away from it. (This is one of the reasons that consultants who analyze data always have work to do.)

The second group is a smaller group of people who enjoy organizing and managing data. This is a very important group of people and most companies and organizations have at least one or two people from this group who play an important, but often ignored role, tending and caring for corporate databases. People from the second group spend a lot of time and effort counting the data and writing reports that summarize the data. In fact, there is whole segment of the software industry that supports people with these tendencies (it is the software segment that includes data warehouses and business reporting software).

The third group is by the smallest and consists of people who develop a deep enough understanding of the data that they can summarize the data statistically and, more importantly, develop statistical models of the data that can be used as a quantitative basis for decision making.

Here are two examples of decisions that benefit from statistical models.

- Your company runs a web site and has an inventory of over 10,000 ads that can be displayed each day in a small text box on the web page. By properly analyzing historical data about the visitors to your web site, you can build a statistical model that can predict the likelihood that a visitor will click on a specific ad. Using this model, you can then offer ads to visitors that are most likely to result in clicks on the ad.

- You live in Chicago and are visiting the art museum on the weekend. You carry four credit cards in your wallet, including one from Citibank. During this visit, Citibank receives a request to approve an authorization for purchase of a flat screen TV from a store in Denver. Should Citibank approve the purchase, decline the purchase, or request more information about the purchase?

Here is an example of a very simple statistical model. Suppose that you are trying to determine whether a credit card transaction is fraudulent or not. To help you do this, you define what statisticians building a model call a *feature*. First, you divide the historical data into two groups: "normal transactions" that are not involved in any fraudulent activities and "fraudulent transactions" which are involved involved in some type of fraud. You then examine the fraudulent transactions and notice that many of them have a lot more transactions at electronics stores with a dollar amount greater than $500 than the normal transactions. Specifically, in this hypothetical example, you notice 7% of the fraudulent transactions have three or more purchases over $500 at electronics stores within fours hours, while only 1% of the normal transactions do. Because of this, you define a feature which is the number of purchases over $500 at stores that sell electronics during the previous four hours.

Suppose now that you are trying to determine whether a certain transaction is suspicious and that it belongs to an account that has 4 transactions at electronics stores during a four hour period. Using this feature you have some evidence that the transaction is fraudulent.

Of course, this model is much too simplistic ever to be of value. On the other hand, with enough features, a statistically valid procedure for determining the constants, such as "3 or more" and "4 hours", and a good mechanism for combining information coming from different features, one could begin to build a good statistical model in this way.

What is important to realize is that although statistical models built in this way may not be very good, they are almost always better than alternative approaches, such as asking an employee at a convenience store to report any individuals that they suspect may have criminal tendencies and are using credit cards in ways they think are suspicious.

In other words, it is almost always better to focus on the question of "Given two statistical models, which one is better," than the question of "Should I go with my business judgment since I know I never make errors or should I use a statistical model built by people with poor social skills that I know has errors." In the era of data, it will be more and more natural to focus on the former question and it will be easier and easier to access the data required to build good statistical models. On the other hand, there will probably always be 100 books explaining how to improve your business judgment for every book explaining how to improve your statistical skills.

One of the things that people find confusing about statistical models is how to measure their accuracy. Here is an example: Suppose a fingerprint is discovered at a crime scene and compared to a database of fingerprints using a methodology (called M) based upon a statistical model for comparing two fingerprints. There are four types of error that can occur:

1. The individual identified from the database actually left the fingerprint at the crime scene. This is called a true positive. The more true positives, the greater the detection rate of the methodology.

2. No individual from the database is identified by M and in fact no individual from the database left the fingerprint at the scene. This is called a true negative.

3. An individual from the database is identified by M, but did not in fact leave the finger at the crime scene. This is called a false positive.

4. No individual from the database is identified by M, but in fact, an individual from the database did leave the fingerprint at the crime scene. This is called a false negative.

All tests have false negatives and false positives. For example, fingerprints are generally presented as being 100% reliable meaning that their false positive and false negative rates are zero. On the other hand, in practice, the rates can be quite different. In 1999, while preparing for the case U.S. v. Byron, an assistant federal public defender in Philadelphia named Epstein Mitchell tested this commonly accepted wisdom.

> [Epstein] showed that standards for examiners vary widely, and that errors on proficiency tests which are given irregularly and in a variety of forms are far from rare. The critical evidence consisted of two fingerprint marks lifted from a car used in a robbery. To prepare for the trial, F.B.I. officials sent the prints to agencies in all fifty states; roughly twenty per cent failed to identify them correctly.
>
> Michael Specter, Do Fingerprints Lie? New Yorker, May 27, 2002.

This is not to say that fingerprints are not effective, but rather that any test in practice has false positives and false negatives and the crucial question is always one of balancing the benefits versus the costs of a test. In many situations, the costs for different types of errors can vary quite a bit. Just think about the impact of convicting the wrong individual based upon a faulty test.

Another important issue is the quality and training of those interpreting tests. The accuracy of tests is usually measured using well-trained experts. Unfortunately, tests are often deployed by individuals with much less training and expertise, which lowers the overall accuracy of the test in practice.

5.14 Case Study: Mammograms

This case study is about using data to make decisions. Some predictions from data turn out to be right and some wrong. Something that almost everyone finds confusing is

	Assertion True	Assertion False
Test Positive	Detection Rate (True Positives)	False Positives
Test Negative	False Negative	Specificity (True Negatives)

Table 5.14: There are four possible outcomes for a test that measures the truth or falsity of an assertion and two types of errors - false positives and false negatives. In the example described above, the assertion is that the fingerprint at a crime scene matches the fingerprints of an individual that is part of a database of fingerprints.

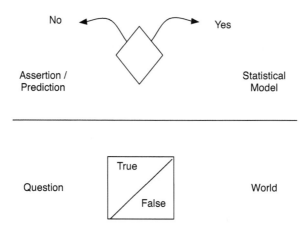

Figure 5.5: This diagram illustrates one way to think about statistical models. Suppose there is a credit card transaction and you are interested in determining whether the transaction is fraudulent or not. In this case, you can think of the statistical model as making predictions, such as whether the credit card transaction is fraudulent.

the different types of errors that arise in this way. This case study looks at the different types of errors that occur with mammograms.

We begin with an excerpt from a CNN article that is available on the web and provides information to help women decide at what age they should begin to have yearly mammograms to screen for breast cancer.

> More false positives. Because mammograms are more difficult to read in younger women, they have a higher incidence of false positives and undergo more unnecessary biopsies. According to the [National Cancer Institute (NCI)], 86 percent of women age 50 and older with an abnormal mammogram turn out not to have cancer. This number jumps to 97 percent in women between the ages of 40 and 49. While it's fortunate that these women turn out to be cancer-free, they still must undergo a painful and perhaps unnecessary procedure to — in most cases — rule out cancer.
>
> More false negatives. There is also a higher rate of false negatives in women younger than 50. The NCI estimates that mammograms miss up to 25 percent of breast cancer in women in their 40s, as opposed to 10 percent for women in their 50s and older. A sense of false security can develop, which may lead to a woman being less vigilant about checking for cancer.
>
> The Mammogram Screening Controversy: When Should You Start? retrieved from cnn.com [31].

The medical study that is the basis for this article was published in the New England Journal of Medicine in 1998 [43] and followed 2227 women over a 10 year period in order to measure the effectiveness of mammograms for screening for breast cancer. A good way to use this type of information as a basis for decision making is to create a diagram like the one in the figure below.

The diagram is read from left to right and consists of nodes that represent groups of individuals and arrows that show how different groups are connected. On the left is a node that represents the number of women in the study (2227 women). On the right are nodes for each of the four possible outcomes of the test. In the middle are branches that divide the women in the study into two groups - those that were diagnosed with breast cancer sometime during the study (88 women) and those that were free of (diagnosed) breast cancer during the study (2139 women).

Looking at the figure below, it is easy to see that of 2227 women who had screening tests, 58 of them had a positive screening mammogram that correctly diagnosed cancer, while 530 of the women had at least one screening mammogram that indicated an abnormality but no breast cancer was present. In other words approximately 10 women had false positives for every woman who was correctly diagnosed with breast cancer by the screening test. This doesn't mean that there is something wrong with the test, but just reflects the fact that all such tests have a certain number of false positives and false negatives.

5.15   Case Study: Events, Profiles and Alerts

In the Data Era, an important question to ask is whether data is at rest or in motion. In prior eras, data was by and large at rest in the sense that data was collected, stored, and then analyzed. The results of analysis were typically written up as reports. For example, in the case study about screening mammograms from the last section, data was collected for ten years, analyzed over a period of months, and an article was then written and published.

In the Data Era, data can also be in motion in the sense that it can consist of a continuous stream of data. In this

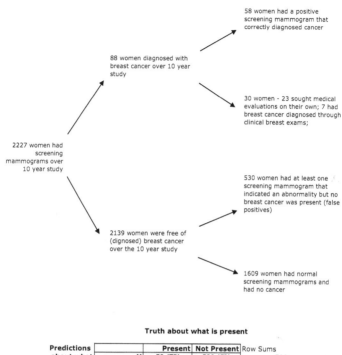

Truth about what is present

Predictions about what is present		Present	Not Present	Row Sums
	Y	58 (TP)	530 (FP)	588
	N	30 (FN)	1609 (TN)	1639
Col Sums		88	2139	2227

Figure 5.6: This diagram illustrates one way to organize false positive and false negative information so that it is easier to understand. The diagram summarizes information about false-positives and false-negatives from a 10 year study of mammograms that were used to screen for breast cancer. The data is from [43].

section, we will discuss streams of discrete events. In the next section, we discuss continuous streams of data, such as those from weather satellites.

With event streams, it is often of interest to process the events as they occur and, if required, to take an action. Events processed in this way are said to be processed in *real time* (although of course there is no such thing as "non-real time.") It is interesting to compare real time automated decision-making with the more familiar example from the prior section, in which data is collected for years, analyzed for months, and decisions are made by trained experts interpreting data.

Streams of event data commonly contain information about one or more entities. Recall that we have discussed events and entities above in Section 5.10. See Table 5.10 for some examples. One way of analyzing these types of events is to consider the events in a window that stretches back to older events (perhaps all the way to the first event) and to construct statistical summaries of the event data, with one summary for each entity. These entity level summaries are sometimes called profiles. In Section 5.10 about the shape of data, we mentioned several examples of these summaries. Here are three of them: clicking on online ads (events) and summaries associated with clicks (user profiles), credit card transactions (events) and summaries associated with transactions (account profiles), and purchasing items at grocery store (events) and summaries about purchases (shopper profiles).

In this section, we will look at another example of streaming event data. This example concerns defending a corporate network from possible cyberattacks. In this example, the events consist of network packets (See Section 3.11) and the summaries consist of information about the IP address which is the source of the packets (IP profiles). The goal is to determine in real time whether the particular IP address is the source of some type of suspicious behavior, perhaps the beginning of an possible network intrusion.

We have mentioned network packets several times. Two

computers on the web typically talk to each other by sending packets of data containing the IP numbers of the source and destination computer, as well as the port number of the source and destination computer. Think of the port number as part of the address - it helps specify exactly where on the destination computer to send the packet. For example, web packets use Port 80 and email traffic uses Port 25.

Sometimes it is useful to think of packets as envelopes — the destination IP and port number are the address, while the source IP number and port number are the return address. Inside the envelope is the payload of the packet (the actual data that is being sent).

In one of the simplest types of attacks, a hostile computer (perhaps because it has been taken over by a moody teenager with too much free time on his hands) sends so many packets that the target computer cannot handle them and crashes. This is called a denial of service attack. These attacks are very simple to detect. A moving window of packets is monitored, summaries are formed, and a statistical model is used to distinguish between normal and abnormal behavior. See Figure 5.7.

For example, most IPs might send a few packets per second, while a denial of service of attack might send 1000 packets or more per second. The goal of a statistical model is to distinguish between these two types of behavior as quickly as possible and to send an alert in real time that can take the appropriate action, such as filtering out all packets from the offending computer. Note that this type of attack can be detected without ever looking at the data, but instead just by building certain statistical profiles obtained by computing statistics in moving windows.

Processing event data to produce summary profiles, analyzing these summary profiles using statistical models, sending alerts in real time, and then taking the appropriate action is emerging as one of the key characteristics of the Data Era.

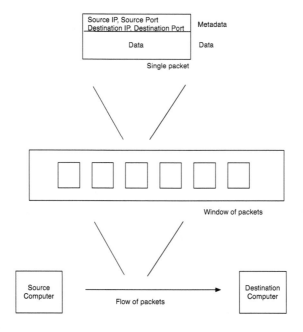

Figure 5.7: This figure illustrates how features are computed statistically from moving windows of TCP packets.

5.16   Case Study: NASA's EOS

Streaming data is of various types, including audio streams, video streams, streams of images, and streams of data from scientific instruments. Perhaps the most familiar type of streaming data are radio and TV broadcasts. Today, most of this streaming data is analog. Over the next decade though, as we enter the Data Era, more and more of this streaming data will be digital, and more and more of it will be captured and archived. A good metric that captures this transition is the amount of streaming video that is watched on computers, tablets and phones versus the amount of video that is watched on televisions.

We now turn to the streaming data provided by NASA's Earth Observing System or EOS. The goal of EOS and related NASA programs is to study the earth as an environmental system by collecting data using satellites and a variety of airborne and ground based instruments. After about a decade of planning, NASA launched the first EOS satellite called Terra in December, 1999.

The Terra Satellite contains several instruments, with names like ASTER, CERES, MISR, MODIS, and MOPITT. Each instrument contains a variety of sensors and each sensor sends a continuous stream of data to earth for processing. From EOS, data is streamed to a NASA ground station in White Sands, New Mexico at a rate of 150 Mb/sec, where it is archived. The data is then streamed from White Sands to several distributed NASA data centers where it is processed to produce dozens of different data products. These various data products are then analyzed by scientists around the world. By the time the EOS program is completed, several petabytes of data will have been collected, processed and archived to produce one of the largest scientific data sets ever created.

The data from Terra is processed to produce a variety of different data sets, such as data sets that include atmospheric temperature, atmospheric water vapor, precipitation, radiation, vegetation, and ocean temperature.

DAAC	Location	Discipline	Instrument
EROS Data Center (US Geological Survey)	Sioux Falls, South Dakota	Land processes data	ASTER, MODIS
Goddard Space Flight Center (NASA)	Greenbelt, Maryland	Upper atmosphere chemistry, atmospheric dynamics, global biosphere, hydrology, and geophysics	MODIS
Langley Research Center (NASA)	Hampton, Virginia	Radiation budget, clouds, aerosols, surface radiation, land processes, and tropospheric chemistry	CERES, MISR, MOPITT
National Snow and Ice Data Center (University of Colorado)	Boulder, Colorado	Snow and ice, cryosphere, and climate	MODIS

Table 5.15: Data streams from on the EOS Terra Satellite via a downlink at 150 Mb/sec to White Sands, New Mexico. From White Sands it is distributed over high performance networks to five sites called Distributed Active Archive Centers or DAACs for further processing. Source: NASA's Earth Observing System [95].

Atmosphere	Aerosols, Air Quality, Atmospheric Chemistry, Atmospheric Phenomena, Atmospheric Temperature, Atmospheric Water Vapor, Clouds, Precipitation, Radiation Budget
Biosphere	Ecological Dynamics, Microbiota, Vegetation
Cryosphere	Sea Ice, Snow/Ice,
Human Dimensions	Environmental Effects
Hydrospere	Surface Water, Snow/Ice
Land Surface	Land Use/Land Cover, Topography
Ocean	Ocean Chemistry, Ocean Heat Budget, Ocean Optics, Ocean Temperature, Ocean Wave, Ocean Wind, Sea Ice, Sea Surface Height, Tide
Radiance/Imagery	Infrared, Microwave, Radar

Table 5.16: The different streaming data products produced by NASA EOS. Source: NASA's Earth Observing System [95].

Today, the collection, processing, and analysis of high volume data streams is an expensive, complex process. Systems take a decade or longer to plan, billions of dollars to operate, and produce petabytes of archived data products. Over the next decade or so, the generation of streaming data by sensors and its processing and analysis will most likely become commoditized.

The cost of sensors, including wireless sensors, has fallen dramatically over the past several decades. Sensors can now be manufactured for a few dollars. Over the next several years, wireless sensors will be commonly attached to a variety of objects, including bridges, cars, trucks, airplanes, and packages.

Each of these sensors will produce a stream of digital data as output. The world will be filled with billions of these inexpensive, wireless sensors, which will be one of the fundamental forces pushing us further and further into the Device Era. The challenge of the Data Era will be to process all this data, extract useful information from it, and use this information to make better decisions.

Over time, we will develop technology that will commoditize the processing of this data and extraction of useful information from it, leading us into the next Era, an era that is not so easy to identify just yet.

Notes

Notes for Chapter 1

The Main Themes. It is obviously an over statement to say that which technology vendors survive over a five year period can best be viewed as a random walk. The perspective of this book is to focus on the underlying structure of the industry as a whole and from this perspective whether Company A, B, or C brings relational databases to market is less important than the fact that once relational database technology is developed it is relatively easy to predict that some company will bring it to market and much harder to predict which company.

Companies themselves can be modeled and these models can be used to predict how likely a company is to remain in the market during the next year. When models like these are built for technology companies, although predictions can be made based upon internal and external factors, it is not a bad approximation over a decade to use a random walk model in which there are probabilities each year that the company will either grow larger, grow smaller, stay the same, or be acquired.

A Billion IP Addresses for Each of Your Children. Routes on the Internet change all the time. Figure 1.1 contains a portion of a traceroute from 2009. As described later in the book, data sent between two computers on the network is divided into what are called packets and these packets are sent from one device to another on the Internet in a series of what are called hops. The Linux traceroute command sends three probes from one device to another. The traceroute commands provides the hop number (column 1 in the figure), the time in milliseconds for each of the three probes (columns 2, 3 and 4), the IP address of the device (column 5), and the Internet address of the device (column 6).

The current Internet uses 32 bits to specify an IP address. The IP address is divided into three components. The first specifies the type (Class A begins with a zero, Class B with a 10, and Class C with a 110), the second the id of the network, and the third the ID of the host or computer. The maximum number of hosts that can be addressed in this way is 2^{32} or about 4 billion, which seemed a lot in 1984 when this scheme was first introduced.

Class	Network	Hosts
0	7 bits	24 bits
10	14 bits	16 bits
110	21 bits	8 bits

The IPv6 scheme uses 128 bits, which can be thought of as divided into eight 16 bit segments. Each 16 bit segment can be written as 4 hexadecimal digits. For example,

FEDC:BA98:7654:3210:FEDC:BA98:7654:3210

is an IPv6 address. The maximum number of hosts that can be addressed in this way is 2^{128} or about 10^{38}, which seems to be a lot today.

Network	Hosts
64 bits	64 bits

The estimates for the world population for 1981 and 2003 are from the US Census web site (www.census.gov). The description of the IPv4 internet protocol is defined in in the DARPA Internet Program Protocol Specification [125]. The description of the IPv6 internet protocol is from [63].

Three Ages of Computing. This description of the alphabetic Greek number system is taken from [112, Hist-Topics/Greek_numbers.html].

The SAD History of Computing. The number system familiar to us is called the Hindu-Arabic number system and requires the symbol zero. The earliest historical evidence for the use of the symbol zero are from 9th Century manuscripts from India [23].

The following two formulas, which were developed in about the 17th century, turn multiplication and division into addition and subtraction:

$$ab = \exp(\log a + \log b)$$

$$a/b = \exp(\log a - \log b)$$

Why Symbols Matter. This section is based in part on [158].

Algorithms as Recipes for Manipulation Symbols. Here is a simple five line Python function to illustrate how square roots can be computed iteratively:

```
def square\_root(a):
    x[0]=a/2.0
    for i in range(1,20):
x[i] = (x[i-1] + (a/x[i-1]))/2.0
print x[i]


x={}
print 'sqrt of 5934939'
square\_root(5934939)
```

Here is another example of an algorithm that generalizes the algorithm for finding square roots discussed in this section. In the 1660's Newton introduced the following simple algorithm for computing the solutions of equations such as $f(x) = 0$. As an example, to find the square root of a, let $f(x) = x^2 - a$. To find the solutions of a quadratic equation, let $f(x) = ax^2 + bx + c$. To find the cube root of a, let $f(x) = x^3 - a$. And to find the solutions of a cubic equation, let $f(x) = ax^3 + bx^2 + cx + d$.

The algorithm depends upon the function $f'(x)$ which Newton introduced and specifies how quickly $f(x)$ changes. For example, if $f(x)$ is a formula for the path of a trajectory, then $f'(x)$ is a formula for its velocity.

1. Take a guess, no matter how bad. Call the guess x_0.

2. Let $x_{n+1} = x_n - f(x_n)/f'(x_n)$,   for $n \geq 0$.

3. If $x_{n+1} - x_n$ is small, stop (the answer is x_{n+1}); otherwise, goto Step 2.

Before Newton's algorithm, there was no simple general method to solve algebraic equations, no matter how good the symbols you had nor how fast the computing device. Newton's algorithm changed all that.

Computing Devices: From Paper to Chips. For more information about the Rhind papyrus, see [12]. For more information about Euclid's Elements, see [44].

Case Study: The Slide Rule. A still useful and influential reference book of mathematical tables is the *Handbook of Mathematical Functions with Formulas, Graphs, and Mathematical Tables* [1]. The handbook is over 1000 pages long and contains a wide variety of different mathematical tables.

For the next few paragraphs we discuss in more detail how the multiplication of two numbers can be computed by adding two related numbers. For example, in a first course in trigonometry, one usually sees the following formula:

$$\sin(A) * \cos(B) = (1/2)\sin(A + B) + (1/2)\sin(A - B).$$

Formulas like these, together with a table of sines and cosines, can be used to reduce multiplications to additions as follows:

1. To multiply a times b, first use a tables of sines to find numbers A and B such that $a = \sin(A)$ and $b = \sin(B)$.

2. Compute $A + B$ and $A - B$.

3. Use the table of sines to find $\sin(A + B)$ and $\sin(A - B)$.

4. Add the two numbers together from Step 3 and divide by 2. By the formula above, this is the desired product of a and b.

In these days of calculators and spreadsheets, it is hard to appreciate why in many cases it is easier to multiply two numbers together using these four steps involving additions and mathematical tables instead of multiplying the numbers directly. Perhaps the best way to understand this is to try one night when you are having trouble sleeping, to multiple the numbers 1.84825884 and 489.83238535 both ways.

Today's logarithm function and its inverse, the exponential function, are quite close to the functions that John Napier introduced in the 16th century. Their are two essential properties of these functions: First, multiplication is reduced to addition:

$$ab = \exp(\log a + \log b).$$

Second, division is reduced to subtraction:

$$a/b = \exp(\log a - \log b)$$

Here exp can be thought of as a function that undoes a logarithm, in the sense that, if in a table of look up values, the logarithm function is the look-up from left to right, then the exp function is the complementary look-up from right to left. These two formulas and a table of logarithms were used to add and multiple numbers for sometime before the invention of the slide rule.

The history of the logarithm is adapted in part from [40]. Information about Edmund Gunter is adapted in part from [112, Biographies/Gunter.html].

From Mainframes to Devices. The quote from Winston Churchill is from a speech he gave to the Royal College of Physicians in London, in 1944. The quote from Ludwig Wittgenstein is from [153, page 1]. For information about the IBM System 360, see [128]. For data about the diffusion of personal computers, see [46].

Case Study: Punch Cards. This case study is adapted from [83].

The Second Era: Desktop Software Applications and the PC. Information about VisiCalc is from [14].

The Fourth Era: Clouds of Devices and Services. It would be convenient if the fourth era had a well recognized name, such as the term "web," which so nicely characterized the third era. Instead, various terms are used today for the fourth era, such as "Device Net" and "EmNet" [100]. Also, sometimes the term "Cloud" is used, although this is generally used for something else [84]. It is still very early in the Fourth Era and I expect a name will catch on before long.

Case Study: Routers In fact, not all computers on the internet have unique IP addresses. First, with the current IP addressing scheme (IPv4), they are simply not enough addresses. Second, for security reasons, many computers are behind firewalls and have IP addresses that are part of private networks. This is not all that different than the telephone system. Telephones that are part of a PBX system usually share a common phone number and are accessed through an extension number.

The example in this section of how routers work is adapted from [154], page 160–164.

Notes for Chapter 2

The Title. The Oxford English Dictionary defines commoditization as a noun with the meaning of commodification. Commodification is defined as "The action of turning something into, or treating something as, a (mere) commodity; the commercialization of an activity, etc., that is not by nature commercial [118]." As used in this Chapter, commoditization is perhaps better defined as "the process by which a good or service transitions from a relatively scarce and expensive item to one that is widely available and inexpensive." In short, items that are commodities are ubiquitous.

Christmas and Easter. Easter Day is often described as the first Sunday after the full moon that occurs next after the vernal equinox [146]. The subtlety is that the full moon in this description is not the full moon as observed by an astronomer but rather an ecclesiastical full moon as determined from tables agreed to by an ecclesiastical council. These tables roughly, but not exactly, follow the astronomical full moon. The reference [146] contains a good description of how these tables work and how they differ from astronomical observations.

Danti's Law - The Commoditization of Time. Meridian lines are describe on page 23 of [73]. Information about the accuracy of various types of clocks and watches is from [107]. Information about the solar year using the calendars of Julius Caesar's, Gregory XIII and Kahan is from [69].

The Commoditization of Space. This section is based upon information about Harrison and his chronometers from the following sources: [129], [67, pages 169–177], and [68, pages 26–29].

Moore's Law – The Commoditization of Processing Power. The quote by Gordon Moore is from a video transcript [94]. The projection is contained in the 1965 Electronics Magazine article [93].

Commoditization is All Around Us. The history of the meter is taken from [68, pages 278–280].

Storage and Johnson's Law. In 2011, you can get a 2 TB disk for less than $100. In 2007, you could buy a Seagate 750 GB Barracuda 3.5 inch Ulta-ATA/100 internal hard drive for $309.00 from Amazon (the retail prices is $399.99). This disk drive has four platters and spins at 7,500 rpm. is 4 inches by 5.8 inches and weighs 1.5 pounds.

The data about disks from mainframe computers is from the Disktrend web site. The first three columns of this table was extracted from www.disktrend.com on June 10, 2002. The remaining columns are computed.

Software and Stallman's Law. Richard Stallman's vision for free software is described in [136]. Stallman is a social activist. A good overview of his social activism can be found on his web site (www.stallman.org).

GNU is an abbreviation for *G*nu is *N*ot *U*nix.

Microsoft's Client Business Unit had $13.2 billion of revenue in 2006 and $12.1 billion of revenue in 2005 [91]. Microsoft's overall revenue for 2006 was $44.3 billion and $39.8 billion in 2005.

In June 2005, Sun Microsystems posted more than 5 million lines of source code from their Solaris operating system as part of an initiative that transforms a proprietary operating system that Sun estimates cost $500 million into an open source operating system called Open Solaris. [138].

A good analysis of how to estimate source lines of code (SLOC) has been done by David A. Wheeler [157]. In particular, the SLOC estimates for the Red Hat Linux distribution are from this paper. This paper also contains the COCOMO estimates. More information can also be found on his web site (www.dwheeler.com/sloc).

The size of the Debian Linux distribution are from the papers [4] and [54]. These references also contain information about the SLOC for the various Microsoft Windows distributions.

There is no agreed upon methodology for measuring

SLOC. Different tools will report somewhat different results. It is especially difficult for an outsider without access to the Microsoft source code to estimate the SLOC. For this reason, all the SLOC of code should be considered approximate, but especially those for the Microsoft Windows systems.

My comments about designs for successful open source software projects is in adapted in part from [152].

Data and the Bermuda Principles GenBank is maintained by the U.S. National Institute of Health. More information about GenBank can be found at the NIH web site (www.nih.gov), which is the source of the information here.

According to the Netcraft Web Server Survey there were 108,810,358 distinct websites in February, 2007. In December 2010, Netcraft estimated that there were approximately 266,848,493 web sites. So assuming that 0.1% of these contained some open data, then there would be over 100,000 sources of open data. This is a very, very rough estimate.

Network Effects.   Since the convention when writing semi-popular books about technology is to make technical assertions, but not always to check them, we will assume in this section, for simplicity, that Metcalf's Law is true.

The quote from Bill Gates is from [48].

For additional material on Metcalfe's Law and network effects, see [116] and [117] and the references contained there.

The list of characteristics of network effects in technology markets is adapted from [131] and [149].

There is no name that I know of to refer to the network effect associated with software and data. In this book I use the names *Linus' Law* and *Pearson's Law* after Linus Torvalds, the the lead developer of Linux, and Karl Pearson, a statistician who lived from 1857 to 1936.

Notes for Chapter 3

A Case Study in Innovation: Approximating Solutions to Equations The Pythagorean Theorem, relating the shorter sides a and b of a right triangle to the longer side c: $c^2 = a^2 + b^2$, is usually one of the first theorems a student learns.

The first known statements of the relation appear on Babylonian tablets dating from the period 1900–1600 B.C. The first proof is thought to be due to Pythagoras (c.560–c.480 B.C.) or to someone from Pythagoras' school. All we know for certain is that the first written proof that is extant is due to Euclid (c. 300 B.C.) Euclid's treatment of this theorem was the standard treatment for hundreds of years.

It is important to remember that the equation as written today is relatively recent: Euclid gave a geometric (not algebraic) statement and a geometric proof.

If we substitute $a = b = 1$ into the equation $c^2 = a^2 + b^2$, then $c^2 = 1^2 + 1^2 = 2$ and c is the square root of 2. More generally to find the square root of a number c, we need to need a solution x to an equation of the form:

$$f(x) = x^2 - c = 0.$$

With this notation, the Newton-Raphson iteration takes the form:

$$x_{n+1} = x_n - f(x_n)/f'(x_n), \qquad n \geq 1.$$

Continuing our example of computing the square root of c using $f(x) = x^2 - c$, we have that $f'(x) = 2x$. More generally, $f'(x)$ is what is called the derivative of $f(x)$ and measures the rate of change of the function $f(x)$.

Here is another example of the Newton-Raphson method. To find a seventh root of a number c, i.e., solutions to the following equation:

$$x^7 = c,$$

you can use the following Newton-Raphson iteration:

1. Begin with a guess, say $x_0 = 1$.

2. Compute

$$x_{n+1} = x_n - \frac{x_n^7 - c}{7x_n^6}, \qquad n \geq 1.$$

3. If x_{n+1} and x_n are close together, stop because you have found the seventh root of c. If not, return to Step 2.

Of course, computers are well suited for computing these types of iterations.

For more information, about the history of the Newton-Raphson algorithm, see [34, page 169].

The simple computer program for computing square roots would never work in practice: First, the program runs into an error if we divide by zero. So we must check for this. Second, sometimes five iterations is enough, sometimes it isn't. We must check for this. Soon we find ourselves with a longer program.

Checking the various different special cases cases quickly takes over as the major task. It turns out that it is easy to leave out various special cases and that as you add more and more cases it becomes easier and easier for them to begin to conflict. This is a simple example of why it is difficult to write even simple programs.

Most computers today follow IEEE Standard 754 for binary floating point arithmetic. Under this standard, floating point numbers are written as +/- d.ddd x 10eee. The number eee is called the exponent and the number d.ddd is called the significand or mantessa. For example, a 32 bit representation for floating point numbers allocates 1 bit for the sign, 8 bits, for the exponent, and 23 bits for the significand. This provides about 8 decimal digits of accuracy for the significand [52].

Even though only 8 decimal digits are significant, the default behavior for simple programs is to write out more than 8 digits after the decimal point. It is important to realize that in general these are incorrect. To get more accuracy, one either needs to use a 64 bit or larger representations for the floating point numbers or to use specialized programs that use variable length representations. With the latter, operations are much slower, but much greater accuracy can be obtained.

A Case Study in Clutter: Business Intelligence. This section was written in 2003. At that time, a key word search using "business intelligence" was done using the online DM Review site www.dmreview.com on March 9, 2003; 1392 documents were returned. A key word search using "business intelligence" was done on Google on March 9, 2003; Google reported that 1,1600,000 were identified containing this phrase. In 2011, a search on Google for "business intelligence" returned approximately 124,000,000 documents containing this phrase.

The Imperative to be in the Upper Right. There are a lot of industries in which a company can choose from in order to be a leader. The U.S. Department of Commerce's book describing the North American Industry Classification System (NAICS) is 1390 pages long [143]. The NAICS uses six digits to identify particular industries: the first two digits designate a business sector, the third digit designates a subsector, the fourth digit designates an industry group, and the fifth digit designates a particular industry. For example, NAICS code 511210 includes packaged computer applications software. See [143] for more details.

Who Clutters. In the Seventh Century B.C.E, standard technology for predicting the future included the entrails of beasts and the motion of the stars. Virgil was a Roman poet who was born in 70 B.C.E, died in 19 B.C.E., and who wrote an epic, which consolidated some of the legends about the ancestors of the Romans. Here is a description of a seer from Book X of his Aeneid [150]:

> Third in the line was Asilas, the mighty seer
> who mediated between men and gods, and who

> knew the secrets held by the entrails of beasts,
> the stars in the sky, the voices of birds, and the
> flash of presaging thunderbolts, ...

Virgil, The Aeneid, Book X, translated by G. R. Wilson Knight [150].

Sources of Clutter: Features. The five page marketing brochure "Crystal Reports XI: Feature Comparison by Version and Edition" contains over 150 features. This brochure was retrieved from the the Business Objects web site on November 20, 2005.

A Case Study in Innovation: Databases. The market research firm IDC estimate of the size of the database market in 2004 was reported in eWeek in the article "Study: 2004 Database Market Grew 12 Percent" [148]. IDC estimated the following worldwide sales of databases as follows: Oracle - $6.2 Billion (41 percent of the market); IBM - $4.59 Billion (31 percent of the market); Microsoft $2.01 Billion (13 percent of the market); Other vendors 2.21 Billion (15 percent of the market).

A brief description of the history of SQL is in [99] pages 162-164.

A Case Study in Innovation: Searching for primes. Since a natural number n always has 1 and n as factors, these are not considered when deciding if a number can be factored into a product of smaller numbers. For example, even though $7 = 1 \times 7$, 7 is still considered to be a prime number. If a number n is not prime it is called *composite* .

Historical facts about Mersenne primes are from [27] and [28], which are excellent resources. The tables listed the large known prime by year from there also. Some of the table entries were computed using a simple Python program.

Here is a Python program for computing primes using the Sieve of Erastosthenes.

```
def sieve(n):
  candidates = range(1, n+1) # [1, ..., n+1]
  candidates[0] = 0   # candidates[0]=1 is not prime
  for p in candidates:
    if p:   # skip zeros
      if p*p>n:
        break   # done
      for q in range(p*p, n+1, p): # sieving
        # candidates[q-1]=q is not prime
        candidates[q-1] = 0
        # return non-zero candidates
        return filter(None, candidates)

# print first n primes
n = 100
print sieve(n)
```

A Python implementation of the Sieve of Erastosthenes.

Lock-In or the Tyranny of Vendors and Users. The discussion of vendor lock in strategies is adopted from [131, Page 117].

A Case Study in Innovation - Routing Packets. Class A, B, and C IP addresses are being replaced by a new approach, which more efficiently allocates the address space called Classless Inter-Domain Routing or CIDR.

Notes for Chapter 4

The Basic Equation of Marketing. Innovators, early adopters, main street, and laggards are well described in [92]. The core ideas are also well described in [38].

How Long to Reach Main Street. The average price for a car in 1914 is from the Cadillac Database [26]. See also [6] and [22]. The corresponding 2003 price was calculated using the US Department of Labor's Bureau of Labor Statistics estimate of the consumer price index of 10.0 for 1914 and 181.7 for 2003 [18]. According to the US Census

Bureau, the US population is about 270 Million, so that using an estimate of 100 Million for the consumer market underestimates its size.

Case Study: The Nike Pagasus. The history about the Nike Pegasus is from the Nike web site [105].

Technology Roadmaps. The table describing the semiconductor roadmap is from the International Technology Roadmap of Semiconductors (ITRS) [66].

Case Study: Grid Computing. The following facts about SETI@home are from a 2002 article about the project [5]. SETI@home was announced in 1998 and the first software was released in May, 1999. By July 2002, over 3.8 million individuals had participated in the project by downloading the SETI@home application and donating cycles to the computation. During the 12 month period starting in July, 2001, the average throughput of the project was 27.36 Teraflops. A Teraflop is a trillion floating point operations per second, such as an addition or multiplication of two floating point numbers. According to the 2002 Top 500 List of the most powerful computers, the SETI@home virtual supercomputer ranked as one of the top ten supercomputers that year [139].

The USA Today article describing shared computing is from [70]. The business week article is from [123]. An excellent introduction to grid computing is the book The Grid: Blueprint for a New Computing Infrastructure [47].

Context. There is no term that I am aware of that refers to factors such as complexity, lock-in and standards that affect the rate at which new technology is adopted by the marketplace. For lack of a better alternative, I use the term *context* in this book.

In [58], the Boston Consulting Group analyzed various markets and pointed out that the top three vendors usually prospered, while the others struggled along.

See [116, page 37] for more discussion about the role of efficiency for inexpensive goods or services.

Forces Effecting Technology Adoption. Information about the growth in the user base of Hotmail is from a Microsoft Press Release [89].

Case Study: Adoption of Relational Databases. The description of the technology adoption of relational databases is based in in part on [99], [55] and [135]. The time line and major events are described in [99, pages 159–169], and [37].

The complexity of querying navigational databases, such as hierarchical and network databases, is described in textbooks on databases, such as [37] and [132].

The number of installations and downloads for MySQL is from the MySQL web site (www.mysql.com).

Case Study: Adoption of Open Source Linux Kernel. The email is from Linus Torvalds [140]. The estimates for the number of Linux users is from [86].

Notes for Chapter 5

Introduction. The quote "Big Data is a Big Deal" is the title of Tom Kalil's March 29, 2012 blog post (www.whitehouse.gov/blog/2012/03/29/big-data-big-deal).

Thinking About Big Data. The study by Peter Lyman and Hal R. Varian about how how much new information is created each year can be found on their web site called "How Much Information? 2003" [82]. The project carefully collected data in 1999 and 2002 and published an analysis of the data in 2000 and 2003. The quote is from their 2000 analysis. In 2003, they revised their 1999 estimate upwards from 1–2 Exabytes to 2–3 Exabytes. It would be nice to include a more recent estimate, but I am not aware of a more recent one that is as authoritative as their 2000 and 2003 studies. The 2003 study contains the estimate that new information from streaming data (such as a person to person telephone call) is about 3-3.5 times larger than the new information from data that is stored on media, such as a hard disk.

Marissa Mayer, the Vice President for Search Products & User Experience at Google, gave a talk at Xerox PARC in Palo Alto California on August 13, 2009 (www.parc.com-/event/936/innovation-at-google.html).

The table illustrating the sizes of kilobytes, megabytes, etc. of storage is adapted from [159].

The Commoditization of Data.   The announcement by Nikon that it is concentrating on manufacturing digital cameras is from January 12, 2006 edition of the New York Times.

The Data Gap.   The data in the first table in this section about earned doctorates is from [103]. The information from the second table about the amount of storage required for different types of multimedia files is from [57].

The British naturalist Charles Darwin lived from 1809 to 1882. The British Penny Post was introduced in 1840. With the Penny Post, a letter could be sent anywhere within England for a penny.

The estimate of 28,800 minutes corresponding to 20 days assumes that a messenger on a horse travels approximately 50 miles per day. Of course, your mileage (carrying data on a horse) may vary.

In December 2004, Google announced that it is working with Harvard University, Stanford University, the University of Michigan, Oxford University and the New York Public Library to digitize the books in their libraries and make them available through Google [17].

Extracting Knowledge from Data.   GenBank is a publicly available database containing genetic DNA sequences maintained by the U.S. National Library of Medicine and National Institute of Health. As of February, 2008 it contained approximately 85,759,586,764 bases from over 260,000 different organisms. See [97] and [9].

Here is the argument that the square root of 2 is irrational. Assume not. In other words, assume that there are integers p and q such that $(p/q)^2 = 2$. Then $p^2 = 2q^2$.

Factor both p and q into a product of primes. Then p^2 is factored into a product of the very same primes as p, but each occurs twice as often in the factorization of p^2 as it does in the factorization of p. Therefore, p^2 has an even number of prime factors. So does q^2. Now since q^2 has an even number of primes, $2 \cdot q^2$ has an odd number of primes (it has just one more). This is a contradiction, q^2 cannot have both an even and an odd number of prime factors. We conclude that the equation $(p/q)^2 = 2$ has no solution for integers p and q. This is the same thing as saying that the square root of two cannot be written as a quotient of two integers and is therefore irrational.

For more information about how simulation is used to study surface temperatures and global warming, see the National Academy of Science report on surface temperature [101].

For the story about why Ulam named the method Monte Carlo, see [61], page 238.

In October, 2004, the International Human Genome Sequencing Consortium, reduced the estimated number of human protein-coding genes from 35,000 to only 20,000–25,000 [111]. Although the number may continue to shrink, our current understanding of the coding of proteins, protein interactions, and metabolic pathways is based upon much more than just genes.

Case Study: Mar's Orbit, Brahe's Data and Kepler's Law Tycho Brahe did not publish his celestial observations, which occupied 17 volumes, but they were used by other astronomers, including Kepler. Brahe's data for the orbit of Mars can be found in [120]. See "A Brief History of Cosmology [114]" for a concise online history of cosmology describing the models of Ptolemy, Copernicus, Brahe, Kepler, and Newton.

Pearson's Law. It seems clear that the value of a column of data grows as it is included in larger and larger collections of other columns, as long as their is a common key for linking different rows in the various columns. On the other hand, whether the value grows linearly, quadratically, or at some other power is not so clear. Odlyzko and Tilly investigated the growth in power of a network containing n sources [117]. They conclude that the power of a network grows more like $n \log n$, rather than the n^2 that occurs in Metcalfe's Law. The same power may very well apply here.

Karl Pearson (1857–1936) introduced a formula for quantifying the correlation between two columns of data and the chi-squared test, both of which are used extensively in statistics. For more information about him, see [124]. Note that if two columns of data are normalized using their mean and standard deviation (into what are called z-values), then the Pearson correlation coefficient of two columns of data is simply the average of the row-by-row product of the columns.

The analysis about voting in Palm Beach County is adapted from [133]. The data is from: election.dos.state.fl.us.

Lessig's Law: Data Just Wants to Be Free The gene (UID 31657232) was obtained from the online GenBank database

http://www.ncbi.nlm.nih.gov/genbank/,

which is maintained by NCBI, which is part of the National Library of Medicine.

The Bayh-Doyle Act or University and Small Business Patent Procedures Act was passed by the U.S. Congress in 1980. Prior to this act, research by a university small business, or non-profit organization that was based upon federal funding could not be easily commercialized since the government retained the ownership of all patents and other intellectual property resulting from the research. This changed with the Bayh-Doyle Act, as the first paragraph of the Act makes clear:

> It is the policy and objective of the Congress to use the patent system to promote the utilization of inventions arising from federally supported

research or development; to encourage maximum participation of small business firms in federally supported research and development efforts; to promote collaboration between commercial concerns and nonprofit organizations, including universities; to ensure that inventions made by nonprofit organizations and small business firms are used in a manner to promote free competition and enterprise without unduly encumbering future research and discovery; to promote the commercialization and public availability of inventions made in the United States by United States industry and labor; to ensure that the Government obtains sufficient rights in federally supported inventions to meet the needs of the Government and protect the public against nonuse or unreasonable use of inventions; and to minimize the costs of administering policies in this area.

U.S. Code 200-212, Title 35, Chapter 18, Patent Rights In Inventions Made With Federal Assistance.

The central dogma of molecular biology is that DNA produces RNA in a process called transcription, and that RNA produces proteins in a process called translation. During the Human Genome Project, it began to be realized that different proteins could be produced from the same genes. For example, it turned out that genes were divided into regions that coded directly for proteins (exons) and regions that do not (introns). By selecting different exons for inclusion, a single gene can produce many different proteins. This is an example of a process called alternate splicing. So even though by the end of the project, the gene count was reduced from about 35,000 to about 26,000, the number of proteins that could be produced from these 26,000 genes was estimated to be much higher than the 35,000 or so proteins than would be produced by 35,000 genes using only the most basic form of translation. By 2004, the estimated number of human genes was reduced further to between 20,000 to 25,000.

BLAST is an abbreviation for Basic Local Alignment Search Tool. BLAST is an algorithm that compares two sequences for similar subsequences [3]. For example, the sequence of a newly identified gene in one organism containing a thousand base pairs can be compared to the entire 4 billion base pairs of the human genome in GenBank.

Case Study: The World Population. The table that estimates the world population at various historical times is from [142].

The Shape of Data. The XML description of the statistical model that classifies an Iris into three types is from www.dmg.org.

Computing statistical profiles while maintaining privacy is an active area of research today. It is important to note that although statistical profiles can be assembled without using *any* personally identifying information, this does not mean that profiles computed in this way cannot be analyzed to reveal personal information. Here is a hypothetical example of how this can occur. Assume that tables of counts are computed that count the number of students that missed 1 day of school, 2 days of school, 3 days of school, etc. Assume that another table of counts contains the average number of days of school missed by students who had various diseases. By putting these two tables together and combining it with some personal knowledge (such as one of your friends missed thirty days of school), you might be able to guess what disease he or she had, especially if there were only a few people in the school that missed that many days of school.

These types of opportunities to identify personal information from summary or aggregated data have been known to be a problem for a long time and is one of the reasons that the U.S. Census only releases information at a fairly high level of summarization.

For more information, about the Google Page Rank algorithm, see [15].

Here is the R code used to compute the page ranks for the example in this section.

```
# initial page ranks
a <- c(0.25, 0.25, 0.25, 0.25)

# number of incoming edges
c <- c(2.0, 1.0, 1.0, 1.0)

# random surfer factor
d <- 0.85

# for simplicity, perform 10 iterations
for (k in 1:10)
{

  a[1] <- (1-d) + d*(a[3]/c[3])
  a[2] <- (1-d) + d*(a[1]/c[1])
  a[3] <- (1-d) + d*(a[1]/c[1] + a[2]/c[2] + a[4]/c[4])
  a[4] <- (1-d)

  wt <- sum(a)
  a <- a/wt

  print(a)
}
```

Case Study: Consumer Credit and Why Not all Databases About 190 Million Americans Are Bad
The data about reported fraud is from the US Federal Trade Commission [144]. The data was retrieved from the web site www.consumer.gov/sentinel on September 1, 2002 for the years 2001, 2002, and 2003; on September 10, 2006 for the years 2004 and 2005; and on March 10, 2008 for the year 2007. The data for 2004 and 2005 was revised when the 2006 data was released. Percentages are computed using

data from [144] and data from Visa about the estimated yearly dollar volume of credit card transactions [151]. Data about the growth in credit consumer credit from 1970 to 2001 is from [141].

Creating Digital Data. For more information about the OdorDB, "Databases for the Functional Analysis of Olfactory Receptors" [36].

Using Data to Make Decisions If a statistical model predicts one of two possible outcomes ($n = 2$) and each outcome can be true or false ($m = 2$), then the number of possible types is four ($4 = 2x2$). More generally, the number of true/false outcomes is $2n$.

Case Study: NASA's EOS. According to an article by Lee Gomes in the Wall Street Journal [53], in August, 2006, there 6.1 million videos, compromising 45 terabytes of digital data, that had been viewed 1.73 billion times. Approximately 50% of the viewers were under 20 years of age. The total time spent viewing the videos was 9,305 years.

References

[1] M. Abramowitz and I.A. Stegun, Handbook of Mathematical Functions with Formulas, Graphs, and Mathematical Tables. U.S. Department of Commerce, 1972.

[2] Alfred Adler, Reflections, Reflections Mathematics and Creativity, The New Yorker, February 19, 1972, p. 39.

[3] S. F. Altschul, W Gish, W Miller, E.W. Myers, and D.J. Lipman, Basic local alignment search tool, Journal Molecular Biology Voluume 215, Number 3, pages 403-10, 1990

[4] Juan Jose Amor, Gregorio Robles and Jesus M. Gonzalez-Barahona, Measuring Woody: The Size of Debian 3.0, Report on Systems and Communications, GSyC, December, 2004, retrieved from libresoft.dat.escet.urjc.es/debian-counting on January 10, 2007.

[5] David P. Anderson, Jeff Cobb, Eric Korpela, Matt Lebofsky, Dan Werthimer, SETI@home: An Experiment in Public-Resource Computing, Communications of the ACM, Volume 45, Number 11, November 2002, pages 56–61.

[6] Automobile Manufactures Association, Facts and Figures, New York, New York, 1950.

[7] Stephen Baker, Google and the Wisdom of Clouds, Business Week, December 13, 2007.

[8] Dennis A. Benson, Ilene Karsch-Mizrachi, David J. Lipman, James Ostell and Eric W. Sayers, GenBank, Nucleic Acids Research, Volume 39, Supplement 1, D32–D37, 2011.

[9] Dennis A. Benson, Ilene Karsch-Mizrachi, David J. Lipman, James Ostell, and David L. Wheeler, GenBank, Nucleic Acids Research, 2008, D25-D30.

[10] Thomas J. Bergin, The History of Computing, 1985, retrieved from www.computinghistorymuseum.org on January 24, 2002.

[11] Tim Berners-Lee, Information Management: A Proposal, May 1990, retrieved from www.w3.org on March 20, 2006.

[12] Carl B. Boyer, A History of Mathematics, Princeton University Press, 1985.

[13] Boston Consulting Group, Perspectives on Experience, 1968.

[14] Daniel Bricklin, Software Arts and VisiCalc, Copyright 2003, retrieved from www.bricklin.com on March 20, 2006.

[15] Sergey Brin and Larry Page, The Anatomy of a Large-Scale Hypertextual Web Search Engine, Stanford InfoLab Technical Report, 1998, retrieved from dbpubs.stanford.edu on September 10, 2005.

[16] Frederick P. Brooks, Jr., The Mythical Man-Month: Essays on Software Engineering Second Edition, Addison Wesley, 1995.

[17] Andreas von Bubnoff, Science in the web age: The Real Death of Print, Nature, Volume 438, pages 550-552, 2005, doi:10.1038/438550a.

[18] US Department of Labor, Bureau of Labor Statistics, retrieved from www.bls.gov on November 14, 2003.

[19] Encyclopedia Britannica, Automotive Industry, www.britannica.com/eb/article?eu=114513. retrieved on July 7, 2002.

[20] Encyclopedia Britannica, Computers, www.britannica.com/eb/article?eu=130076, retrieved on August 18, 2002.

[21] Encyclopedia Britannica, Euclidian Geometry, www.britannica.com/eb/article-235561, retrieved on March 12, 2006.

[22] Encyclopedia Britannica, Motor Cars, Volume 15, page 881, Encyclopedia Britannica, Inc., Chicago, 1957.

[23] Encyclopedia Britannica, Numerals and Numeral systems, www.britannica.com/eb/article-233818 retrieved on February 2, 2006.

[24] Encyclopedia Britannica, Transportation, History of, www.britannica.com/eb/article?eu=120012. retrieved on July 7, 2002.

[25] Vannevar Bush, As We May Think, The Atlantic, July, 1945.

[26] Yann Saunders, The Cadillac Database, retrieved from http://www.car-nection.com/yann/ on November 10, 2003.

[27] Chris Caldwell, The Largest Known Prime by Year: A Brief History, retrieved from http://primes.utm.edu on December 23, 2001.

[28] Chris Caldwell, Mersenne Primes: History, Theorems and Lists, http://primes.utm.edu on September 12, 2002.

[29] M. Campbell-Kelly, M. Croarken, R. Flood and E. Robson, editors, The History of Mathematical Tables: From Sumer to Spreadsheets, Oxford University Press, 2003.

[30] Chao-Kuei, Categories of Free Software, Free Software Foundation, 2001. Retrieved from /www.gnu.org/philosophy/categories.html on March 8, 2002.

[31] The Mammogram Screening Controversy: When Should You Start? www.cnn.com, September 27, 1999, retreived from cnn.com on Dec 10, 2006.

[32] M. Collett, T. S. Collett, S. Bisch, and R. Wehner, Local and global vectors in desert ant navigation, Nature 394, pages, 269 - 272, 16 July 1998.

[33] E. F. Codd, A Relational Model of Data for Large Shared Data Banks, Communications of the ACM, Volume 13, No. 6, June 1970, pages 377-387.

[34] Jean-Luc Chabert, editor, A History of Algorithms, Springer-Verlag, Beidelberg, 1999.

[35] Francis S. Collins, Michael Morgan, Aristides Patrinos, The Human Genome Project: Lessons from Large-Scale Biology, Science, Volume 300, page 286-290, 2003.

[36] C. J. Crasto, N. Liu and G. M. Shepherd, Databases for the Functional Analyses of Olfactory Receptors, Neuroscience Database: A Practical Guide, Rolf Kotter, editor, Kluwer Academic Publishers, Dusseldorf, 2003, pages 37–50.

[37] C. J. Date, An Introduction to Database Systems, Addison Wesley Longman, 7th edition, 1999.

[38] William H. Davidow, Marketing High Technology, Free Press, New York, 1986.

[39] Chris DiBona, Sam Ockman, and Mark Stone, Open-Sources, Voices from the Open Source Revolution, O'Reilly, Cambridge, 1999.

[40] Dr. Anthony, Logarithms: History and Use, retrieved from www.mathforum.org on November 1, 2004.

[41] Stephen Donadio, The New York Public Library: Book of Twentieth-Century American Quotations, New York, Stonesong Press, 1992.

[42] Jack Dongarra and Francis Sullivan, Guest Editors' Introduction: The Top 10 Algorithms, Computing in Science and Engineering, Volume 2, Number 1, IEEE Press, 2000.

[43] Joann G. Elmore, Mary B. Barton, Victoria M. Moceri, Sarah Polk, Philip J. Arena, and Suzanne W. Fletcher, Ten-Year Risk of False Positive Screening Mammograms and Clinical Breast Examinations, New England Journal of Medicine, Volume 338, pages, 1089-1096, 1998.

[44] Euclid, The Thirteen Books of the Elements, Translated with introduction and commentary by Sir Thomas L. Heath, Second Edition Unabridged, Dover Publications, Inc., New York, 1956.

[45] Christopher Farrell, A Better Way to Size Up Your Nest Egg: Monte Carlo models simulate all kinds of scenarios, Business Week, January 22, 2001.

[46] Mark Doms, FRBSF Economic Letter 2005-37, The Diffusion of Personal Computers across the U.S., Federal Reserve Bank of San Francisco, December 23, 2005.

[47] Ian Foster and Carl Kesselman, The Grid: Blueprint for a New Computing Infrastructure, Morgan Kaufmann Publishers, Inc., San Francisco, California, 1999.

[48] Bill Gates, The Road Ahead, Penguin Books, 1995.

[49] Categories of Free and Non-Free Software, Free Software Foundation, 2001, retrieved from http://www.gnu.org/philosophy/categories.html on March 8, 2002.

[50] George Gilder, Metcalf's Law and Legacy, Forbes ASAP, September 13, 1993. Also, George Gilder, Telecosm, Simon and Schuster, 1996. Also, George Gilder, Telecosm: How Infinite Bandwidth Will Revolutionize Our World, Free Press, 2000.

[51] Gerd Gigerenzer, Calculated Risks, Simon and Schuster, New York, 2002.

[52] David Goldberg, What Every Computer Scientist Should Know about Floating-Point Arithmetic, ACM Computing Surveys, Volume 23, Number 1, 1991, pages 5-48.

[53] Lee Gomes, Will All of Us Get Our 15 Minutes ON a YouTube Video, Wall Street Journal, August 30, 2006.

[54] Jess M. Gonzlez-Barahona, Miguel A. Ortuo Prez, Pedro de las Heras Quirs, Jos Centeno Gonzlez, Vicente Matelln Olivera, Counting potatoes: The size of Debian 2.2, http://people.debian.org/ jgb/debian-counting/counting-potatoes

[55] Jim Gray, Data Management: Past, Present, and Future, retrieved from research.microsoft.com/ gray on December 20, 2001.

[56] Eric Lee Green, Commoditizing Computers, retrieved from www.badtux.org on December 20, 2002.

[57] Brian Hayes, Terabyte Territory, American Scientist, Volume 90, Number 3, 2002, pages 212-216.

[58] Bruce D. Henderson, The Experience Curve — Reviewed, Boston Consulting Group, Inc., 1973.

[59] John L. Hennessy and David A. Patterson, Computer Architecture: A Quantitative Approach, second edition, Morgan Kaufmann Publishers, Inc., San Francisco, California, 1996.

[60] David G. Hicks, The Museum of HP Calculators, www.hpmuseum.org. Retrieved on March 10, 2003.

[61] P. Hoffman, The Man Who Loved Only Numbers: The Story of Paul Erdos and the Search for Mathematical Truth, New York, Hyperion, 1998.

[62] Internet Assigned Numbers Authority (IANA), IPv6 Address Allocation and Assignment Policy, retrieved from http://www.iana.org/ipaddress/ipv6-allocation-policy-26jun02 on December 26, 2003.

[63] Internet Engineering Task Force (IETF), IP Version 6 Working Group (ipv6), retrieved from www.ietf.org on December 10, 2003.

[64] Internet Engineering Task Force (IETF), RFC 2460, IPv6 Specification, retrieved from www.ietf.org on December 10, 2003.

[65] Internet Software Consortium, http://www.isc.org/.

[66] International Technology Roadmap of Semiconductors (ITRS), retrieved from http://public.itrs.net on November 23, 2003.

[67] Cedric Jagger, The World's Great Clocks and Watches, Hamlyn, London, 1997.

[68] James Jespersen and Jane Fitz-Randolph, From Sundials to Atomic Clocks, Dover Publications, Mineola, New York, 1999.

[69] William Kahan, Computing Days Between Dates, the Day of the Week, etc. Retrieved from www.cs.berkeley.edu/ wkahan/daydate/daydate.txt on September 10, 2002.

[70] Michelle Kessler, High tech's latest bright idea: Shared computing, USA TODAY, January 8, 2003.

[71] Rachael King, How Cloud Computing Is Changing the World, Business Week, August 4, 2008.

[72] Ray Kurzweil, The Age of Spiritual Machines, Penguin Books, New York, New York, 1999.

[73] J. L. Heilbron, The Sun in the Church, Harvard University Press, Cambridge, Massachusetts, 1999.

[74] Alan Hall, How the Web Was Wove, Business Week, October 5, 2000.

[75] Projects Prove Innovation, InfoWorld, November 20, 2001.

[76] Internet Software Consortium, Domain Survey, retrieved from www.isc.org on August 10, 2002.

[77] Barry M. Leiner, Vinton G. Cerf, David D. Clark, Robert E. Kahn, Leonard Kleinrock, Daniel C. Lynch, Jon Postel, Larry G. Roberts, and Stephen Wolff, A Brief History of the Internet, Internet Society, 2000, retrieved from www.isoc.org/internet/history/index.shtml on January 4, 2002.

[78] Michael Lesk, How Much Information is there in the World, retrieved from http://www.lesk.com/mlesk/ksg97/ksg.html on December 20, 2001.

[79] Lawrence Lessig, The Future of Ideas: The Fate of the Commons in a Connected World, Random House, New York, 2001.

[80] Steve Lohr and John Markoff Windows Is So Slow, but Why?, New York Times, March 27, 2007.

[81] Peter Lyman and Hal R. Varian, How Much Information?, retrieved from www.sims.berkeley on June 30, 2001.

[82] Peter Lyman and Hal R. Varian, How Much Information? 2003, retrieved from www.sims.berkeley on November 20, 2006.

[83] David L. Margulius, When PC Still Means 'Punched Card', New York Times, February 7, 2001.

[84] Peter Mell and Tim Grance, The NIST Definition of Cloud Computing, NIST Special Publication 800-145, 2011.

[85] Scott McCartney, ENIAC: The Triumphs and Tragedies of the World's First Computer, Walker Publishing Company, 1999.

[86] Josh McHugh, For the lover of hacking, Forbes Magazine, August 10, 1998.

[87] Donella H. Meadows, Dennis I. Meadows, Jorgen Randers, and William W. Behrens III, The Limits to Growth, Club of Rome, 1972.

[88] Gregory John Michaelson, Undusting Napier's Bones, retreived from http://www.macs.hw.ac.uk/ greg/calculators/napier/ on August 10, 2003.

[89] MSN Hotmail Continues to Grow Faster Than Any Media Company in History, Microsoft Press Release, February 8, 1999. Retrieved from www.microsoft.com on July 10, 2002.

[90] Microsoft .NET, retrieved from www.microsoft.com on February 10, 2002.

[91] Microsoft Corporation Annual Report, 2006.

[92] Geoffrey A. Moore, Crossing the Chasm, Harper-Collins Publishers, New York, 1991.

[93] Gordon E. Moore, Cramming more components onto integrated circuits, Electronics, Volume 38, Number 8, April 19, 1965.

[94] Moore's Law, An Intel Perspective, video transcript, retrieved from www.intel.com on June 11, 2009.

[95] NASA's Earth Observing System, retrieved from www.nasa.gov on March 10, 2002

[96] NOAA/NASA AVHRR Oceans Pathfinder Program, retrieved from www.nasa.gov on March 10, 2002.

[97] National Center for Biotechnology Information, GenBank, www.ncbi.nlm.nih.gov/Genbank, 2008.

[98] National Research Council, An Assessment of Space Shuttle Flight Software Development Processes, National Academy Press, 1993.

[99] National Research Council, Funding a Revolution: Government Support for Computing Research, National Academy Press, 1999.

[100] National Research Council, Embedded, Everywhere, National Academy Press, Washington, D.C., 2001.

[101] Committee on Surface Temperature Reconstructions for the Last 2,000 Years, Surface Temperature Reconstructions for the Last 2,000 Years, National Research Council, The National Academies Press, Washington, DC, 2006.

[102] National Academy of Engineering, Greatest Engineering Achievements of the 20th Century, 2000.

[103] US National Science Foundation, Division of Science Resources Studies, Survey of Earned Doctorates, 2004, retrieved from NSF on June 10, 2006.

[104] Netcraft Web Server Survey, retrieved from www.netcraft.com on May 10, 2007.

[105] Nike - Our history, retrieved from www.nike.com on June 10, 2002. Nike - Our chronology, retrieved www.nike.com on June 10, 2002.

[106] Who Needs High-Accuracy Timekeeping and Why?, NIST Press Release, December 29, 1999, retrieved from www.nist.gov on September 20, 2006.

[107] National Institute of Standards and Technology, A Walk Through Time, retrieved from www.nist.gov on July 25, 2002.

[108] Nikon Plans to Stop Making Most Cameras That Use Film, New York Times, January 12, 2006.

[109] Nokia, Quarterly and Annual Information, retrieved from www.nokia.com/2008/Q1/index.html on June 10, 2008.

[110] Human Genome Project Information, retrieved from www.ornl.gov/hgmis/project/hgp.html on January 3, 2002.

[111] Human Genome Product Information, How Many Genes Are in the Human Genome?, retrieved from www.ornl.gov on June 10, 2006.

[112] John J O'Connor and Edmund F Robertson, The MacTutor History of Mathematics Archive, retrieved from www-history.mcs.st-andrews.ac.uk on March 6, 2006.

[113] John J O'Connor and Edmund F Robertson, Greek Number Systems, in [112].

[114] John J. O'Conner and E. F. Robertson, The Mac-Tutor History of Mathematics Archive, retrieved from www-gap.dcs.st-and.ac.uk/ history/ on June 20, 2003.

[115] John J. O'Conner and E. F. Robertson, Mathematics and Architecture, in [112].

[116] Andrew M. Odlyzko, The history of communications and its implications for the Internet, June, 2000, retrieved from http://www.research.att.com/ amo/doc/networks.html on July 1, 2001.

[117] Andrew Odlyzko and Benjamin Tilly, A refutation of Metcalfe's Law and a better estimate for the value of networks and network interconnections, retreived from www.umn.edu on June 10, 2006.

[118] Oxford English Dictionary, Oxford University Press, Second Edition, 1989.

[119] Tim O'Reilly, The Open-Source Revolution, Release 1.0, November, 1998.

[120] Wayne Pafko, Visualizing Tycho Brahe's Mars Data, retrieved from www.pafko.com on June 20, 2003.

[121] Percedes Pascual, Xavier Rod, Stephen P. Ellner, Rita Colwell, Menno J. Bouma, Cholera Dynamics and El Nio-Southern Oscillation, Science, Volume 289, 2000, pages 1766–1769.

[122] Byron E. Phelps, Early Electronic Computer Developments at IBM IEEE Annals of the History of Computing, Volume 2, Number 3, July, 1980.

[123] The Party-line Approach to Supercomputing, Developments to Watch, BusinessWeek, December 5, 1994.

[124] Theodore M. Porter, Karl Pearson: The Scientific Life in a Statistical Age, Princeton University Press, 2004.

[125] Jonathan B. Postel, Darpa Internet Program Protocol Specification RFC792, September, 1981, Retrieved from http://www.rfc-editor.org on December 10, 2003.

[126] Jonathan B. Postel, Simple Mail Transfer Protocol, August 1982, RFC 821, retrieved from www.rfc-editor.org on February 2, 2002.

[127] Price Waterhouse Coopers, PWC Internet Survey, retrieved from www.pwcinternet.com on September 8, 2000.

[128] Emerson W. Pugh, Lyle R. Johnson and John H. Palmer, IBM's 360 and Early 370 Systems, MIT Press, Cambridge, 1991.

[129] John Harrison and the Longitude Problem, Royal Observatory Greenwich Online Exhibit, www.rog.nmm.ac.uk/museum/harrison, retrieved on July 5, 2002.

[130] Jean E. Sammet, Brief Summary of the Early History of COBOL, IEEE Annals of the History of Computing, Volume 7, Number 4, 1985.

[131] Carl Shapiro and Hal R. Varian, Information Rules, Harvard Business School Press, Boston, Massachusetts, 1999.

[132] Avi Silberschatz, Michael Stonebraker, and Jeff Ullman, editors, Database Systems: Achievements and Opportunities, Communications of the ACM, Volume 34, Number 10, pages 110–120, 1991.

[133] Richard L. Smith, A Statistical Assessment of Buchanan's Vote in Palm Beach County, retrieved from www.stat.unc.edu on June 10, 2006.

[134] Michael Specter, Do Fingerprints Lie?, New Yorker, May 27, 2002.

[135] Paul McJones, editor, The 1995 SQL Reunion: People, Projects, and Politics, retreieved from www.mcjones.org on January 24, 2002.

[136] Richard Stallman, The GNU Manifesto, Free Software Foundation, 1985 and 1993, retrieved from www.gnu.org on March 8, 2002.

[137] Sun Microsystem Corporate History, retrieved from www.sun.com on December 31, 2001.

[138] Sun Microsystems, No-cost Software FAQs, retrieved from www.sun.com on January 10, 2007.

[139] The Top 500 Supercomputer Sites, retrieved from www.top500.org on Oct 10, 2008.

[140] Linus Torvalds, Linux History, July 31, 1992, retrieved from www.li.org on October 10, 2002.

[141] Michael Turner, The Fair Credit Reporting Act: Access, Efficiency & Opportunity; The Economic Importance of Fair Credit Reauthorization, Information Policy Institute, 2003.

[142] U.S. Census Bureau, World POPClock Projection, retrieved from http://www.census.gov.

[143] U.S. Department of Commerce, North American Industry Classification System (NAICS), 2007.

[144] US Federal Trade Commission, Consumer Sentinel, retrieved from www.consumer.gov on September 1, 2002, September 10, 2006 and March 10, 2007.

[145] US Federal Trade Commission, Prepared Statement of the Federal Trade Commission on the Fair Credit Reporting Act Before the Senate Committee on Banking, Housing, and Urban Affairs Washington, D.C. July 10, 2003.

[146] U.S. Navel Observatory, The Date of Easter, retrieved from www.navy.mil on December 10, 2006.

[147] Hal R. Varian, How Much Does Information Technology Matter?, New York Times, May 6, 2004.

[148] Lisa Vaas, Study: 2004 Database Market Grew 12 Percent, retrieved from www.eweek.com on March 7, 2005.

[149] Cento G Veljanovski, Competition Law Issues In the Computer Industry: An Economic Perspective, QUT Law and Justice Journal, Volume 3, Number 1, 2003, pages 3–27.

[150] Virgil, The Aeneid, translated by G. R. Wilson Knight, Penguin Books, London, 1956.

[151] Visa, About Visa USA, retrieved from http://www.visa.com on August 29, 2003.

[152] Paul Vixie, Software Engineering, in DiBona, 1999, op. cit., pages 91–100.

[153] G. H. Von Wright, editor, Culture and Value, translated by Peter Winch, The University of Chicago Press, 1980.

[154] Jean Walrand and Pravin Varaiya, High Performance Communication Networks, Second Edition, Morgan Kaufmann, San Francisco, California, 2000.

[155] David A. Wheeler, The Most Important Software Innovations, May, 2001. Retrieved from http://www.dwheeler.com/ on July 7, 2001.

[156] David A. Wheeler, Estimating Linux's Size, July 26, 2001, Version 1.05, Retrieved from http://www.dwheeler.com/ on August 10, 2002.

[157] David A. Wheeler, More Than a Gigabuck, Estimating GNU/Linux's Size, July 2002. Retrieved from http://www.dwheeler.com/ on August 10, 2002

[158] Michael R. Williams, A History of Computing Technology, Prentice-Hall, 1985.

[159] Roy Williams, Data Powers of Ten, retrieved from www.davedoyle.com on May 20, 2006.

[160] Richard Saul Wurman, Information Anxiety, Bantam Books, New York, 1990. See also, Richard Saul Wurman, Information Anxiety 2, QUE, Indianapolis, 2001.

Index

air cushioning, 132
algorithms, 15
alphabet, 14, 205
Andreesen, Marc, 90
ASCII, 204
atomic clocks, 45
average selling price, 123

Bermuda Principles, 75, 189
Berners-Lee, Tim, 90
big data, 163
Bill's Law, 69, 127
Bowerman, Bill, 131
Brahe, Tycho, 179
breakthrough, 138
breast cancer, 213
business intelligence, 88

calendars, 47
chasm, 125
Cisco, 36
cloud computing, 139
clusters, 137
clutter, *see* market clutter
COCOMO cost model, 70
Codd, E. F., 107, 147
coding
    odors, 206
    text, 204
commoditization, 3, 53

CPUs, 52
of data, 43
space, 50
storage, 64
time, 45
competition, 93
computer
    hollowed out, 35
    tapes, 104
computing
    cloud, 139
    clusters, 137
    context, 140
    data era, 161
    epochs, 10
    era, *see* era, 24
    grid, 139
    integration, 142
    lock-in, 140
    platforms, 38
    roadmap, 134
    standards, 140, 144
concordance, 204
consultants, 97
credit card fraud, 209
credit scores, 199
cycle stealing, 139

Danti's Law, 47
Darwin, Charles, 169

data
    commoditization, 166
    era of big data, 5
    event streams, 196
    gap, 168
    graph, 197
    how much, 166
    open, 189
    semi-structured, 194
    sequence, 194
    shape of, 193
    size of, 162
    streaming, 216, 219
    tabular, 182
data mining, 87
data transport
    by horse, 169
database, 145
    adoption, 145
    distributed, 108
    keys, 107
    navigational, 147
    relational, 107
    schema, 106
    System R, 148
    tables, 146
    transaction, 106
denial of service attack, 217
devices, 8
    computing, 23
doubling criterion, 58
doubling game, 58

early adopters, 123
El Nino, 183
email, 31
epicycles, 178
era

clouds of devices, 34
computing, 3, 9
data, 43
mainframe, 26
pc, 28
web, 30
Euclid, 109

false negative, 213
false positive, 211, 213
FCRA, 199
features, 92
fingerprints, 211

Galileo, 175
Gates, Bill, 78, 127
GenBank, 75, 189
geometric growth, 58
Gilder's Law, 66
Gilder, George, 66, 77
GIMPS, 111
GNU Manifesto, 72
GPS, 49
graph, 197
grids, 139

Harrrison, John, 51
host ID, 7
Human Genome Project, 75,
        176, 189, 196

images
    digital vs analog, 168
information anxiety, 88
innovation, 3
    changing perception, 89
    rarity of, 82
IP address, 5, 116
IPv6, 6

Iterative methods, 85

Johnson's Law, 62
Joy, Bill, 127

Kepler,Johannas, 179
KKR, 30

laggards, 123
law
    Bill's, 69
    Gilder's, 66, 79
    Johnson's, 62
    Linus's, 79
    Metcalfe's, 77
    Moore's, 52
    Pearson's, 75
    Stallman's, 67
Lessig, Lawrence, 188
Linux, 156
lock-in, 140
longitude, 51

Main Street Market, 123, 127
market
    clutter, 4, 82, 96, 98
    forces, 121
    leader, 94
    submarkets, 92
    vertical, 93
marketing
    basic equation, 123
mathematical tables, 20
meridian line, 47
Metcalfe's Law, 66, 77
Metcalfe, Robert, 77
Model T, 144
Monte Carlo algorithms, 176
Moore's Law, 52

Mosaic, 136
mythical man-month, 158

network
    effects, 77, 79
    ID, 7
    latency, 57
    local area, 36
    packets, 217
    telephone, 111
Newton, Isaac, 83, 180
Newton-Raphson Method, 85
Nike, 130
number
    as limit, 87
    as solutions to equations,
        84
    prime, 109
    rational, 174
    viewed as lengths, 83
    viewed geometrically, 13

Occam's razor, 179
open source software, 70, 159

Page Rank, 198
Pearson's Law, 182
PMML, 194
primes, 109
    Mersenne, 110
profiles, 216
Ptolemaic convenience, 179
punched cards, 27, 104
Pythagoras, 83, 174

real time, 216
relational database, see database
research
    applied, 135

basic, 134
resources
    controlled vs free, 188
roadmap, 134
router, 36, 114
routing tables, 118
ruler and compass construc-
        tions, 84

SAD, 10, 22
satellites, 219
schema, 106
science
    data, 173
    experimental, 175
    simulation, 176
sensors, 222
Sieve of Eratosthenes, 110
slide rule, 10, 19
SMTP, 32
Stallman's Law, 73
Stallman, Richard, 67
standards, 140, 144
statistical model, 209
    errors, 210
Sun Microsystems, 128
symbols, 10, 11

technology
    adoption cycle, 4, 40
    context, 120
    roadmap, 120, 134
telephones, 113
Torvalds, Linus, 156
transforming technologies, 61

VisiCalc, 29
von Neumann, John, 91

waffles, 132
winners, technology, 91

About the Author

Robert L. Grossman is a faculty member at the University of Chicago and a Partner of Open Data Group. At the University of Chicago, he is the Director of Informatics at the Institute for Genomics and Systems Biology, a Senior Fellow at the Computation Institute, and a Professor in the Division of Biological Sciences. He founded Open Data Group in 2002, and since then it has been one of the leaders in building predictive models over big data.

Cover design by Rachel Pasch. Cover image by Michal Sabala.

27346075R00155

Made in the USA
Lexington, KY
28 December 2018